OSPREY

# Napoleon's Imp
# Headquarters (2)

## On campaign

Ronald Pawly · Illustrated by Patrice Courcelle

First published in Great Britain in 2004 by Osprey Publishing
Elms Court, Chapel Way, Botley, Oxford OX2 9LP, United Kingdom
Email: **info@ospreypublishing.com**

CIP data for this publication is available from the British Library

ISBN 1 84176 794 8

Editor: Martin Windrow
Design: Alan Hamp
Index by Glyn Sutcliffe
Originated by Grasmere Digital Imaging, Leeds, UK
Printed in China through World Print Ltd.

04 05 06 07 08    10 9 8 7 6 5 4 3 2 1

FOR A CATALOGUE OF ALL BOOKS PUBLISHED BY
OSPREY MILITARY AND AVIATION PLEASE CONTACT:
**NORTH AMERICA**
**Osprey Direct, 2427 Bond Street, University Park, IL 60466, USA**
Email: **info@ospreydirectusa.com**

**ALL OTHER REGIONS**
**Osprey Direct UK, P.O. Box 140, Wellingborough,**
**Northants, NN8 2FA, UK**
Email: **info@ospreydirect.co.uk**

**www.ospreypublishing.com**

## Acknowledgements

The author wishes to thank Mr David Chevalier for redrawing the map of Napoleon's tented camp (see page 41) after the contemporary drawing kept at the National Archives in Paris.

## Artist's Note

Readers may care to note that the original paintings from which the colour plates in this book were prepared are available for private sale. All reproduction copyright whatsoever is retained by the Publishers. All enquiries should be addressed to:

Patrice Courcelle, 33 avenue des Vallons, 1410 Waterloo, Belgium

The Publishers regret that they can enter into no correspondence upon this matter.

This early portrait by Riesener, 1806, of an *adjutant-commandant* of the Imperial Guard in full dress, illustrates the richly gold-embroidered buttonhole loops of those staff officers with the status of field officers of the line. The coat was dark blue with, by regulation, scarlet collar and cuffs, although dark blue facings were also seen. This officer's pair of heavy bullion epaulettes identify his rank as the equivalent of colonel; the aiguillettes indicate service with the Imperial Guard, and his buttons would show a crowned eagle. (Courtesy Musée de l'Empéri/former Brunon collection, Salon de Provence, France)

## INTRODUCTION

THE FIRST PART of this study discussed and illustrated the composition, organization and functions of the various departments and offices of Napoleon's Imperial Headquarters – the *Grand Quartier Général Impérial*. This comprised his Military and Civil Households, and the separate Army General Headquarters – *Grand État Major Général* – presided over for much of the duration of the Empire by Marshal Berthier, Napoleon's 'Major-General' or Chief of the General Staff.[1]

This second part describes the reduced staff which accompanied Napoleon in 1814 and 1815; and describes the practical experience of the Emperor's headquarters in the field. We have chosen to do this principally through the example of the 1815 Waterloo campaign, but with back-references to compare various aspects with earlier stages of the Empire. We also present some further details of the layout of the Emperor's tented camps in the field, which will be new to most English-speaking readers; and illustrate a further selection of the uniforms worn around the Imperial Headquarters.

\* \* \*

The daily routines followed by Napoleon when on campaign are only sparsely covered in the best known contemporary memoirs written about his life and career. However, some members of his immediate entourage did leave us glimpses of how he travelled, lived, ate and conducted his daily life in the field – among them, his valets Constant, Marchand, Roustam and Ali; his Grand Equerry, Gen Caulaincourt; and Gen Guyot, the commander of the Mounted Chasseurs of the Imperial Guard.

The popular engravings printed during or after his reign leave us with one physical image of the Emperor above all – that of a stocky figure, deep in thought, wearing a plain grey overcoat and small *chapeau*. The familiarity of this image is not surprising, since at some periods of his reign he spent more time on campaign with his armies than he did in Paris. For example, in 1805 he spent more than six months away from his capital; in 1807, 1808 and 1809, eight months; in 1812, seven and a half months; and in 1813, more than six months.

---

1 See Elite 115, *Napoleon's Imperial Headquarters (1): Organization & Personnel* – where explanations of the functions of the various officials of the Households and General Staff, mentioned below in this text, will also be found.

While life in his palaces was organized according to one of th
strictest etiquettes of any court in Europe, most of this ceased to app
from the moment he left their gates, only to be reinstated when h
settled down for a longer period – as for example at Finkenstein in 180
and Dresden in 1813. When in bivouacs Napoleon became a soldi
once again, and he felt at ease among his troops. For the final campaig
in 1815 the organization and routines were largely unchange
although on a smaller scale than in earlier years.

# 1814

In 1814 Napoleon was forced, for the first time since the 1790s, to fig
within the borders of France herself; and despite the despera
circumstances this will be remembered as one of his finest campaigns. Th
grandeur of his former might – as demonstrated during the Russia
campaign in 1812, and celebrated at his birthday parade in Dresden on
August 1813 – was gone, and for the first time in years his decisions we
constrained by the reduced strength of his army. In that sense the ma
who had made himself an emperor had become simply a general agair
His entourage was organized accordingly and, together with Marsh
Berthier's Imperial General Staff, it still functioned efficiently despite th
severe losses suffered since 1812.

Leaving Paris to join his army on 25 January 1814, the Emperor w
accompanied by the Grand Marshal of the Palace, Gen Henri-Gatie
Bertrand. General Bertrand was now responsible not only for the Civ
Household, but had also taken over the duties previously performed k
the Grand Equerry, Gen Armand de Caulaincourt; the latter was no
serving as Minister of Foreign Affairs and trying to save France throug
negotiation.

The *aides de camp* to the Emperor who left Paris with him were Ger
Drouot – also serving as Major-General of the Imperial Guard – Flahau
Corbineau and Dejean. The orderly officers were Gourgauc
Mortemart, Montmorency, Caraman, Pretet, Laplace, Lariboisière
Lamezan and Desaix. Count de Turenne still acted as First Chamberlai
and Master of the Wardrobe; Baron de Canouville served as Marshal c
the Palace, and Baron Mesgrigny was the Equerry. The Emperor'
private Cabinet was still manned by his secretary Baron Fain, and Baro
Yvan followed the Emperor as First Surgeon.

Others in the Emperor's reduced staff were the Cabinet clerk
Jouanne and Rumigny; the secretary-translator Lelorgne d'Ideville; th
engineer LtCol Atthalin and geographical engineer Lameau, bot
working in the Emperor's topographical office; the Chevaliers Fourrea
and Vareliand, respectively physician and surgeon to the imperial staf
and finally the *fourriers du Palais* Baillon and Deschamps.

For personal service Napoleon could rely upon his private valet
Constant, Pelart and Hubert, and the faithful Mameluke, Roustam
*piqueur* (outrider) Antoine Jardin, who had once fulfilled this functio
in the stables of Versailles under King Louis XVI; and *maître d'hôte
(kitchen controller) Colin. Most of these trusted servants, who ha
followed their Emperor on nearly all his campaigns, had already left fo
Châlons to prepare for Napoleon's arrival.

Although his conduct of the 1814 campaign was a magnificent example of his sheer brilliance in the manoeuvring of troops, Napoleon was seriously outnumbered, and severely handicapped by the losses suffered in Russia and since by his cavalry, and among the army's experienced regimental officers and NCOs. He succeeded in holding the Allies at bay for a while, even beating them on more than one occasion; but France was war-weary, and so were many of her marshals and administrators. Finally defeated, and with Paris capitulated, Napoleon retreated to Fontainebleau where, one by one, those to whom he had given titles, riches and palaces abandoned him.

General Caulaincourt had been sent off to treat for terms with the victors, but nothing would satisfy them except the Emperor's abdication. Left with neither a throne nor an army, Napoleon was unable to give favours; many high-ranking officers and administrators no longer had any motive for attaching themselves to his destiny, and started offering their services and loyalty to the returning Bourbon monarchy of King Louis XVIII.

Marshal Berthier, still acting as Major-General, received the overall command of the army, and ordered the General Headquarters, commanded by Bailly de Monthion, to go to Chartres. Berthier also took care of organizing the detachments of the Imperial Guard that would accompany Napoleon into exile on the Mediterranean island of Elba.

Travelling non-stop between Paris and Fontainebleau, Berthier was blamed for having abandoned his benefactor. However, Berthier was still looking after the wellbeing of the army, after Napoleon himself had authorized his troops to serve the king. Later, Berthier would present himself at the head of the marshals before Louis XVIII, saying that France, 'having groaned for the last 25 years under the weight of the

At noon on 20 April 1814 the imperial carriages entered the Cour du Cheval Blanc at Fontainebleu. At 1pm the Emperor left his apartments, and was surrounded by the remaining members of a court once brilliant and numerous. Still with him were Maret, the Duke of Bassano; Count de Turenne; Gens Belliard and Fouler; Cols Belly de Bussy, Montesquiou, and Atthalin; Barons Mesgrigny, Fain, de la Place and Lelorgne d'Ideville; Chevalier Jouanne; and two Polish officers, Gen Kosakowski and Col Vonsowitch. Napoleon shook hands with them, then descended the stairs and walked past the coaches towards the Grenadiers of the Guard. He addressed them, and kissed their regimental flag. This was his last act before leaving for Elba. (Collection Alfred & Roland Umhey, Germany)

misfortunes which oppressed her, was no
looking forward to the happy day which shon
upon her'. This speech was considered l
hardcore Bonapartists as showing ingratitud
towards the Emperor. When King Louis made h
public entry into Paris, and Berthier was see
riding in front of the carriage in all the pomp c
his new situation, reproachful voices shouted: 'G
to the island of Elba, Berthier! Go to Elba!'

However, Berthier was far from alone in disa
pointing expectations that he would follow th
Emperor into exile. According to the memoirs c
Planat de la Faye, former ADC to Gen Drouot, th
same was true of the First Orderly Officer, Cc
Gourgaud. His many public expressions of h
love, gratitude and loyalty to the Emperc
suggested that he would accompany Napoleon t
Elba. On the evening before he was due to set sa
for the tiny new kingdom, Gourgaud aske
Napoleon's permission to go and visit his mothe
to bid her farewell; but he never returned.

Many who had the most to lose had starte
changing sides at the earliest opportunity, an
others simply retired to their homes in order to await a final settlemer
of the new government; but some still displayed unlimited dedication t
their old master. One of them, the ADC Gen Charles de Flahaut, wrot
on 8 April 1814:

'The Emperor would have granted everyone the freedom to serv
under the new government. But how could we serve it, when our flags ar
adorned with mourning bands, and when we feel a righteous disdain fc
the hatred borne against us? I will follow the Emperor to his destination;
believe that I must, and have no second thoughts where my duty
concerned. When, at the end of all these events – all these betrayals, all th
infamy (according to one side), all these glorious deeds (according to th
other) – we have become untouchable (irreproachable), we may fin
happiness at last… '

The following day Flahaut wrote to his mother, Mme de Souza:

'I have not yet resigned, and since you wish me to – in spite of th
mourning covering our flags, in spite of the shameful humiliation of ou
homeland – I shall once more wear my uniform and serve my countr
I have served it well during all these events. I have helped save it fror
civil war, even against my own best interests. But what is personal intere
compared to that of the homeland? I would have given my life to save
from the humiliation to which it has stooped…'

'I shall stay here until the Emperor leaves. I would even accompar
him to the place of his banishment, should he so wish. Afterwards, I sha
return to you. I have asked him (believing it to be my duty) for h
opinions about and his intentions for the conduct of those that were mo
dear to him. *"As I wish to retain your esteem, Sire, I would gladly obtain fror
you rules of conduct that only Your Majesty can give me."* He replied that h
*"would like to see us happy; that all that opposed our happiness would be again*
*his intentions; that all this was over, and that each man must serve his country.*

In a letter to his mother, Flahaut wrote: 'I think I shall accompany the Emperor, perhaps to the border, perhaps to the place he must live in. It is a duty I shall accomplish, for misfortune will not keep me from him. He had thought about me and had wished to keep me close to him. I replied that I answer to you before all. All the insults heaped upon him in the public papers bring me closer to him. Recently, I have spent most of my nights in his company, and never before have I witnessed such calm, such courage. *"I regret nothing"*, he told me; *"and I would have been more unfortunate had I signed any treaty that would have robbed France of even one village in her possession, since the day that I vowed to maintain the integrity of her territory."'*

After this First Abdication, Napoleon left Paris for the island of Elba on 20 April 1814, parting from his last faithful servants, including Maret, Duke of Bassano, and Gens Bertrand and Belliard; Cols Belly de Bussy, A.Montesquiou and Gourgaud[2]; Count de Turenne, Gen Fouler, Baron de Mesgrigny, and the imperial secretary Baron Fain.

Even in the petty state that he created on Elba, its sovereign wished to keep the former splendour of his Parisian palace, the Tuileries. With this in mind he reorganized his Military and Civil Households, even commissioning local citizens as orderly officers,[3] and retaining the imperial dark green uniform.

Back in France, his followers gathered in Bonapartist salons like those of Queen Hortense and Duke Maret. These were kept under surveillance by the secret police, and reports were duly filed – such as one concerning the former ADC Flahaut, written on 22 December 1814:

'He is still a young man… He keeps company with most of the generals who are distinguished by their devotion to Napoleon. General Exelmans, one of his closest friends, visits him quite often. General Flahaut also maintains relations with Generals Marchand and Belliard and with Marshal Pérignon. He sometimes sees Marshals Marmont, Ney, Oudinot and Davout. He presents himself at Court only infrequently. Together with his step-father, the Count de Souza, he has paid a few visits to the British ambassador [the Duke of Wellington]. He frequently visits the Duchess de Saint Leu… General Flahaut strongly manifests his attachment to King Murat; one should not have any doubts whatsoever about his bad intentions towards the present government…'

# 1815: REINSTATEMENT OF THE HOUSEHOLDS

After his escape from Elba and his return to the Tuileries in March 1815, Napoleon reinstated his Military and Civil Households; and from early in the Hundred Days most of the essential bureaux were in readiness to accompany him on campaign. The Military Household still consisted of ADCs to the Emperor with the rank of general, and their personal ADCs (known as *petits aides de camp*); orderly officers to the Emperor; and a topographical bureau.

---

2 Gourgaud is represented on the right hand side in Vernet's painting *Napoleon's farewell at Fontainebleu*; this is in contrast to the testimony of ADC Planat de la Faye, quoted above.
3 These were B.Bernotti, B.de Binetti, P.de Pérez, L.de Pons, F.Senno & R.Z.Ventini, all commissioned 15 May 1814; and J.Roul, commissioned 23 August. All were dismissed as orderly officers on 30 March 1815, but several continued to serve the Emperor.

## The Military Household:
## Aides de camp to the Emperor

*General of Division Count A.C.F.Lebrun*, a 40-year-old cavalry officer and ADC since June 1800, was the elder son of the Imperial Arch-Treasurer the Duke of Plaisance.

*General of Division Count J.B.J.Corbineau*, 39, a cavalry officer appointed ADC on 26 January 1813. On the very dark night of 30 January 1814 after the battle of Brienne, Napoleon was returning to his HQ at Maizières when his small entourage was suddenly attacked by a group of Cossacks. His immediate companions were Gens Dejean and Corbineau, *Chef d'escadron* Gourgaud and Marshal Berthier (who jumped into a ditch). While Dejean shouted for assistance, Corbineau and Gourgaud covered the Emperor, who was threatened by a Cossack lance. Reacting swiftly, the orderly officer Gourgaud killed the Cossack with a pistol shot – an action that was rewarded with a colonelcy.

*General of Division Count C.A.J.Flahaut de la Billarderie*, a 30-year-old officer of engineers, appointed ADC on 24 October 1813. It was said of Flahaut, one of the great charmers of his age, that he was in fact a natural son of Talleyrand and Mme de Souza. Later, his love affair with Napoleon's step-daughter Hortense – daughter of Josephine, and former Queen of Holland as wife of Napoleon's brother Louis – resulted in a child who would be known as Charles Auguste Louis Joseph Count, later (in 1862, under the reign of his half-brother Napoleon III), Duke of Morny. Flahaut would follow the Emperor to Paris during his retreat from Waterloo.

*General of Division Count P.F.M.A.Dejean*, a 35-year-old cavalry officer appointed ADC on 20 March 1813. His father had been the Minister for War Administration between March 1802 and January 1810.

*General of Brigade Baron Simon Bernard*, 36, an engineer officer appointed ADC on 21 January 1813. With Baron d'Atthalin acting as commander of engineers at the fortress of Landau in 1814, Bernard would replace him as director of the Emperor's topographical office.

*Maréchal de Camp C.A.F. Huchet, Count de Labédoyère*, 29, appointed ADC on 26 March 1815. In March 1815 Labédoyère left Grenoble at the head of his regiment, the 7th Line Infantry; and at Vizille he offered it to the returning Napoleon – the first military unit to rally to the Emperor after his escape from Elba. Later this fluent Flemish speaker was sent secretly into Belgium to investigate the mood of the Belgian people; he also travelled between the different Allied areas of occupation to discover their strengths and locations. Labédoyère's report was influential in Napoleon's decision to attack towards the crossing of the River Sambre at Charleroi.

Other ADCs who served at Corps level were:

*General of Brigade Count A.Drouot*, 41, an artillery officer appointed ADC on 26 January 1813 – also known as 'the Sage of the Grande Armée'. He was *aide-major-général* of the Army of the North, but from 15 June he served as interim commander of the Imperial Guard, replacing Marshal Mortier, who fell ill after an attack of sciatica.

*General of Brigade Count L.M.Letort*, a 42-year-old dragoon officer, appointed ADC on 21 April 1815. He commanded the Mounted Dragoons of the Imperial Guard, replacing Gen Count P.Ornano. Charging with the Imperial Guard duty squadrons at Gilly on 15 June, he suffered wounds from which he died at Charleroi two days later.

*General of Brigade G.Mouton, Count of Lobau*, 45, an infantry officer, and an ADC since 6 March 1805. At the battle of Aspern-Essling in May 1809 he had covered the French retreat from the island of Lobau with great courage and success. In 1815 he commanded VI Corps of the Army of the North.

*General of Brigade Count C.A.L.A.Morand*, a 44-year-old infantry officer appointed ADC on 23 March 1815, commanded the Foot Chasseurs of the Imperial Guard.

*General of Brigade Count H.C.M.J.Reille*, 40, an infantry officer and an ADC since 13 May 1807. He commanded II Corps in 1815, at Thuin, Marchienne-au-Pont, Lodelinsart, Gosselies and the battles of Quatre-Bras and Waterloo.

The average age of the Emperor's ADCs in 1815 was thus 39 years; those serving as full time aides averaged 35, and those who held posts with the army averaged 43 years old.

## Orderly officers to the Emperor

The orderly officers were considered as the 'youngsters' *(gamins)* of Napoleon's Imperial Headquarters; except for their leader Col Gourgaud, who was 32, the orderly officers were between 25 and 30 years old. In 1805–06 the Emperor had 'borrowed' orderly officers from Berthier for his own employment. Napoleon was a man of habit, however, and disliked seeing new faces around him all the time; he therefore decided to create his own corps of orderly officers (as described in the previous part of this study). In 1815, they were as follows:

*First Orderly Officer, Col G.Gourgaud*, who had returned to his post on 3 April 1815, and who would be promoted *maréchal de camp* on 21 June. Gourgaud would follow Napoleon into final exile on St Helena.

*Captain C.H.Baston Count de la Riboisière*, a former imperial page, who was commissioned on 22 April 1815.

*Captain Planat de la Faye*, commissioned on 22 April 1815. This artillery officer would not serve at Waterloo, as he was sent on a mission to Gen Bressinet's 27th Infantry Division in the Pyrenees, only hearing the news of the defeat on returning to Paris. He tried to follow Napoleon into exile, but was held prisoner on Malta.

*Captain P.H.Amillet*, commissioned on 22 April 1815. Later in his career this engineer officer would become head of the Paris fire brigade.

*Captain A.M.E.Regnauld de Saint Jean d'Angély*, son of a Minister of State and a cavalry veteran of Russia, Leipzig and the 1814 campaign. Commissioned on 2 May 1815, during the Waterloo campaign he commanded the duty squadrons, a function held before the First Abdication by the 2nd Colonel of the Mounted Chasseurs of the Imperial Guard. After Waterloo he would serve on the staff of the Imperial Guard until 17 July 1815.

*Captain H.D.J.de Lannoy*, a former ADC to Gen de Labédoyère, who received his commission on 22 April 1815.

General J.L.F. Count Le Marois (1776–1836), who was appointed an ADC to Gen Bonaparte in 1795. Clearly a man of strong character, he was against the idea of an invasion of Russia in 1812, and served during that whole campaign as commander-in-chief of the Camp de Boulogne, in order to discourage any English invasion attempt. In 1813 he became commander-in-chief of the troops in Westphalia and governor of Magdeburg. During the Waterloo campaign he commanded the 14th and 15th Military Divisions at Rouen, where he was reorganizing the National Guard at the time of the Second Abdication. (Collection du Musée National du Château de Malmaison, France)

*Captain Alfred de Montesquiou*, the third son of 'Maman Quiou' governess of Napoleon's son, the King of Rome, *Gouvernante des enfan[...] de France* ('Governess of the Children of France') and wife of the Gran[...] Chamberlain. Alfred, a cavalryman, received his commission on 2 Ma[...] 1815.

*Sub-lieutenant M.M.Autric*, of the 31st Mounted Chasseurs of the Line. A[...] a *demi-solde* (half pay officer) he was one of the first to rally to th[...] Emperor when he returned from Elba, resulting in his commission a[...] orderly officer on 15 March 1815.

*Captain J.J.A.Chiappe*, a native of Ajaccio, Corsica; this engineer becam[...] an orderly officer on 18 May 1815, and lost a finger at Waterloo.

*Chef d'escadron A.P.Moline de Saint Yon*, a former ADC to Gen Reille. A[...] ADC to Gen Brayer he went to meet the Emperor at Grenoble on [...] March 1815 to reassure Napoleon of the Lyon garrison's loyalty, an[...] received his commission three days later. In 1845 he would becom[...] Minister of War.

*Captain J.Dumoulin* of the National Guard. By profession a glov[...] manufacturer in Grenoble, he had corresponded with his old frien[...] Emery, who was surgeon of the Elba battalion. From time to time he se[...] parcels of gloves, in the seams of which he hid secret messages for th[...] Emperor. When Napoleon returned Dumoulin was rewarded with th[...]

**Napoleon used his personal ADCs for long and detailed tours of inspection on his behalf; he mainly employed his orderly officers (right) to inspect units, places, or regions where he intended to conduct operations. Their expensive silver-embroidered sky-blue uniforms are illustrated on Plate C, Elite 115. (Collection Alfred & Roland Umhey, Germany)**

The Marquis de Vence as an orderly officer to Napoleon, after a painting by Albrecht Adam in 1809. Here we see the typical sky-blue and silver uniform worn from that year forward, except that his light cavalry shabraque shows some kind of Austrian knot in the rear corner. Albrecht Adam was not the sort of artist to invent such details; we should accept that even with the strictest regulations regarding uniforms, some personal touches were possible, especially among officers with wealth and connections. (Author's collection)

rank of captain and, at his request, was made an orderly officer on 12 March 1815. Present at Waterloo, he was wounded by a sabre cut that rendered him deaf, and was taken as a prisoner of war to Britain.

*Captain M.J.L.d'Y de Résigny* was a cavalryman, former staff officer and ADC to Gen Lebrun, and later *petit aide de camp* to the Emperor. He was commissioned orderly officer on 22 April 1815. After the Second Abdication he tried to follow Napoleon into exile, but was held prisoner from August 1815 in Fort Manoel on Malta, together with Gens Savary and Lallemand (both of whom escaped on the night of 5 April 1816), Cols Planat, Résigny and Schultz (who were sent to Gozo), Mesurier, Auric and Rivière. Later Résigny would marry Marshal Ney's widow.

*Captain Saint Jacques* of the artillery, who was commissioned on 22 April 1815.

Two artillery colonels, V.Belly de Bussy and A.Laurent, also served as supernumeraries with the Military Household.

The former had been a fellow student of Napoleon at the La Fère artillery school. Unsympathetic to Revolutionary ideas, he had emigrated, but returned to France after the Peace of Amiens and became mayor of his native village of Beaurieux (Aisne). During the 1814 campaign Belly de Bussy offered his services to the Emperor, and

The Polish Count Adam Désiré Chlapowski (1788–1879) served as an orderly officer to the Emperor from 9 May 1808 until 13 January 1811. Here he is represented in a uniform of the same style as the 1809 sky-blue dress, but in green with gold embroidery – perhaps a transitional style between the original much plainer green and the final sky-blue designs? Another contemporary portrait of a Swiss officer shows a scarlet uniform with gold embroidery – scarlet was traditional for Swiss troops in Napoleon's army. (Author's collection)

served as guide at Craonne on 6–7 March. Napoleon rewarded him with the officer's cross of the Legion of Honour, commissioned him as an ADC, and promoted him to the rank of artillery colonel. Belly de Bussy served at the battles of Rheims (13 March 1814), Arcis-sur-Aube (19 March) and Saint Dizier (24 March). Slightly wounded at Waterloo, he was still able to follow Napoleon towards Paris.

Colonel Albert Laurent commanded the 1st Foot Artillery Regiment at the time of Napoleon's return from Elba. On 5 June 1815 he received orders to join the Imperial Headquarters of the Army of the North at Laon. There he received the command of the auxiliary horse artillery battery of the Young Guard. However, since this unit was not entirely formed he was commissioned to serve as an ADC to the emperor.

As in the past, the Military Household also contained a topographical office, now commanded by Gen Bernard, and a 'historical office' or bureau of archives.

## The Civil Household

The Emperor's Civil Household also saw some changes in 1815, but was still under the command of Gen Bertrand, Grand Marshal of the Palace, and Gen Caulaincourt, Duke of Vicenzo, who had initially resumed his functions as Grand Equerry. The latter was soon re-appointed as Minister of Foreign Affairs, however, and this post so absorbed him that on 10 June 1815 he was temporarily replaced in the Household by J.P.Bachasson, Count of Montalivet and the Crown Intendant-General. Montalivet's service was brief; he lacked the necessary experience, and with little time to organize the Emperor's transport Caulaincourt put forward the seasoned Gen A.E.Fouler to replace him.

Albert-Emmanuel Fouler, Count de Relingue (1769–1831), was the son of the former Master of the Royal Stables at Versailles. Following in his father's footsteps, he developed a keen interest in horses and started his career as a royal stable boy. In September 1787 he entered the army as a sub-lieutenant, soon rising to lieutenant and captain (1792). After serving throughout the Revolutionary Wars and commanding the 11th Cuirassiers, Fouler joined the Imperial Household as Master of Horse to the Empress in May 1804. He served at Austerlitz and Jena; was commissioned general of brigade on 31 December 1806, and was taken prisoner by the Austrians at Essling in 1809. After his release he was recalled to Paris to become one of the Emperor's equerries, a position that he never in fact took up: on 17 April 1810 he became Master of Horse, with responsibilities for the Imperial Stables. This included the procuring of horses, their training, care and maintenance – a task that kept him in France for the next four years, his military career taking second place.

When the Allies brought the war within the borders of France, Fouler offered his services to the Emperor in the field and joined his staff. He distinguished himself at Saint Dizier on 23 March 1814, and was promoted general of division the following day. When Napoleon returned in 1815, Fouler offered his services once again and was reinstalled as Master of Horse, replacing Caulaincourt. Without an effective military command, he followed the Emperor and his staff, always keeping fresh horses at hand. During Waterloo he kept a number of spare mounts at Le Caillou, and it was these that carried the Emperor and his immediate suite to safety during the retreat. Fouler retired from the army on 9 September 1815 and returned home to Lillers, never to serve again.

In 1815, Gen Fouler was ably assisted by one Gy, a 'horse team quartermaster', who was also a confidant of Caulaincourt. Together with the equerry Count de Canisy, Fouler would swiftly organize the Emperor's field train *(Service d'expédition)*; and on 10 June 1815 the detailed order of march was ready. The Emperor's train would consist of a convoy of 14 carriages, with each place assigned to a member of the staff or Cabinet or a servant; these were to leave the palace in three different groups. The rest of the imperial baggage was, as before, divided into heavy and light trains. The heavy *(Gros bagages)* was composed of wagons and carriages; the light *(Service léger)*, of a large number of mules, skilfully handled by some 30 valets, each of them mounted on a mule with a portemanteau in front of him on the mule's neck. Each valet led by a pair of reins a second mule, carrying two leather-covered boxes attached by means of a pack saddle. In these boxes were provisions, silver plates and cutlery, bottles, decanters, coffee cups, etc., all marked with the imperial emblem. A mount in the *piquets* of spare horses was now reserved for Gen Fouler instead of the Grand Equerry, one for the Mameluke Ali instead of Roustam, and one for Surgeon Lameau instead of Yvan. In addition to these 13 horses in total, there were remounts for the staff officers who had to follow the Emperor closely, and even for the Major-General.

For his own personal service the Emperor relied upon six close attendants. Louis J.N.Marchand, replacing Constant since the First Abdication, was responsible for the Emperor's clothes and dressing, meals and ablutions – duties that occupied him from the moment when Napoleon rose until he finally went to bed.

Louis E.Saint Denis, known as 'Ali', acted as Napoleon's personal Mameluke. Like Constant, his former and better-known Mameluke Roustam had left his service in 1814. Roustam's former assistant Ali now took his place, with a variety of tasks. He followed the Emperor everywhere, inside and outside the palace, and – as Roustam had done – he slept in front of Napoleon's bedroom door.

The Emperor's former private doctor, Yvan, had left Napoleon after the latter's suicide attempt at Fontainebleau. He was now replaced by Dr Lameau; and Baron Dominique Larrey, chief surgeon of the Imperial Guard, was also attached to the personal service of the Emperor.

The last two attendants were the pages who would follow the Emperor on campaign, named Gudin and Cambacérès. They might be employed as orderlies to carry messages, or as equerries in case the latter were serving elsewhere.

A typical view of Napoleon travelling in France. His coaches were mainly driven by postilions, but his Mamelukes – Roustam, and later Ali – sat on the front seat. The black box-like structure between Roustam's seat and the cabin was part of the special design of the *dormeuse*, housing drawers, cupboards, and an extending section so that the Emperor could stretch out to sleep in his carriage. The postilions' costumes are illustrated on Plate B. (Painting by Eugène Lelièpvre, collection Alfred & Roland Umhey, Germany)

# 1815: THE EMPEROR ON CAMPAIGN

With the political situation in France rather unstable, and faced by the implacable hostility of an entire European coalition, Napoleon had to take the initiative with a *coup de main*, opening almost the only offensive campaign of his career. He had the Dutch-Belgian, British, Prussian, Austrian and Spanish against him, and Russia too was mobilizing an immense army to march towards France.

## Departure

On the eve of every new campaign, the time of departure remained known only to the Emperor himself; but when the order to leave was given it no longer came as any surprise, since it had all happened so often before. By this stage everything was in readiness for the final decision; all the ministries had their instructions, and all current problems had been dealt with. At the palace, postilions and coachmen were waiting, carriages were standing ready, and horses bridled and saddled. Boxes and trunks for baggage were packed and ready to be closed on the last-minute items. The only thing that was awaited was the final order to leave. A concert or ball might detain Napoleon, or perhaps he was still working in his Cabinet, sorting out his paperwork; but the moment would come when a bell suddenly sounded.

Napoleon's valet Marchand entered the office, and the Emperor commanded: 'I leave at four o'clock'.[4] From the moment the servant

4  Marchand was responsible for the *nécessaire de voyage*. Made by the famous goldsmith Biennais, this mahogany and ebony box measured 52cm long by 36cm wide and 18.5cm deep (20.5 x 14 x 7.25 in), and contained no fewer than 112 selected items for the Emperor's paperwork, toilet and meals.

hut the door behind him, activity in the palace accelerated to a whole ew tempo. The peaceful offices suddenly became a beehive: duty fficers ran up and down the corridors, and secretaries packed their apers, counted maps, and closed their portfolios. In the courtyards ne heard the sound of valets loading boxes on the carriages, grooms nd servants clattering about, shouting and swearing. When the clock ounded four, everything was ready, and the door of the Emperor's oach stood open. The Emperor appeared, and without delay mounted is coach, followed by the Grand Marshal. The Mameluke Ali took his lace on the front box and two valets at the back, and the postilions' hips urged the teams into motion, setting the convoy on the road for ne distant Imperial Headquarters where the Major-General and his taff were awaiting his arrival. When the sound of the last carriage rinding over the cobblestones had faded away, the palace went back to leep; the next day courtiers would be surprised to discover that the mperor had departed.

Only a few days earlier, sometimes even hours, a selected group of nembers of the different household departments had been sent head to prepare accommodations for the journey. Relay stations with pare horses, all guarded by Imperial Guard troops, were organized long the road the Emperor was to take. There they had to wait for his rrival; sometimes this could take one or several days, or even weeks, epending upon the political situation and on the timing of Japoleon's final decision.

When the Emperor was staying for longer than one or two nights at the same place, then the requirements of imperial palace etiquette would apply. Here we see the advance members of his Mounted Chasseurs escort followed by two *piqueurs* (outriders) of the imperial stables in full dress uniform. (Collection Alfred & Roland Umhey, Germany)

The full dress of the *piqueurs,* in imperial green with gold lace decoration. Their full dress sword looked more like a hunting weapon than an épée; their shabraques were red, edged with gold. See also Plate D1, Elite 115. (Collection Paul Meganck, Brussels)

V. HUEN

### Travel

The speed with which Napoleon travelled from one place to another wa astonishing. For the Austerlitz campaign of 1805, he left his palace at S Cloud on 24 September before 5am; at 9am on 1 October he arrived a Ettlingen in Germany. For the 1806 campaign in Prussia and Poland h departed from St Cloud at 4.30am on 25 September, crossing the Rhin at Mainz three days later. In 1808 he left Rambouillet for Spain at 4am on 30 October, and arrived at Tolosa at 6am on 4 November. For th 1809 campaign against Austria he left Paris at 4.30am on 18 April, and was in Strasbourg two days later. Yet another departure from St Clou was recorded at 4am on 15 April 1813; on that occasion he arrived i Mainz at around midnight on the 16th. On his way to join his armies th carriages and the state of the roads set the speed, but still the Empero pushed them to surpass these limitations. On 18 July 1807 he wrote t the Empress that he had not left his coach for the last 100 hours.

On campaign the duty outriders, like the rest of the Household servants, wore a more comfortable and practical costume. The green coat is laced with gold on the stand-and-fall collar, the double cuffs and the pocket flaps, and is worn over a red waistcoat; white summer breeches are shown here, with 'jockey' boots, and the hat is plain black. (Collection Paul Meganck, Brussels)

Napoleon's itineraries reveal his astonishing energy. After the battle of Wagram in 1809, he left Passau at 9am on 20 October. Travelling the whole day and the next night, he arrived at Nymphemburg at 8.45am on the morning of the 21st – and went hunting… At 5am on the 22nd Napoleon left for Augsburg, where he attended Mass, had breakfast with the bishop, and again spent the whole of the next night in his carriage, to arrive in Stuttgart at 7am on the 23rd. There he watched a spectacle that the King of Wurttemberg had ordered in his honour, leaving only at 10pm for Strasbourg. At midday on 24 October he left that city, to breakfast at Marshal Oudinot's castle at Bar-le-Duc at 10am the next morning. Passing by Epernay, his journey ended at the palace of Fontainebleau at 9am on 26 October. Nobody was present to receive him, since they had not expected him until the evening of the 27th.

The same happened when he left Valladolid in Spain on 16 January 1809, arriving at the Tuileries at 9am on the 23rd, when everybody thought that he was still on the other side of the Pyrenees. Sometime he travelled so fast that after arriving at his destination he had to wait for his secretaries, the equipment of his Cabinet or even a change of clothes to catch up with him.

One of Napoleon's most astonishing movements was his return from Russia. At 10pm on the night of 5 December 1812 he mounted his carriage at Smorgoni; the next day at 2am he left Oschmiana, stopped at Vilna, and arrived at 5am on 7 December at Kovno. At Gragov he changed his carriage for a sledge, which he shared with the Grand Equerry. Two days later they were at Pultusk, and at Warsaw by 11am on 10 December. At Goglau they changed the sledge for a carriage and pushed forward towards Dresden, where they arrived on 13 December at midnight. By 7am the next morning they had already left the Saxon capital; two days later they were at Mainz, and arrived at the Tuileries at 11pm on 18 December, where the Emperor immediately started making preparations for the next day.

Sometimes his stages were so long, fast and improvised that it became impossible for the Mounted Chasseurs escort to keep up, and a carefully selected group of them was chosen to follow the Emperor . For instance, on 29–30 May 1813 they travelled 200 miles; on 2 June, 100 miles; and shortly afterwards another 80 miles. On 7 June, after 19 hours on the road with only a short halt to eat, Napoleon's escort and their commander fell out one by one, leaving the Emperor alone with his immediate staff.

**The Emperor's coach halted in bad weather to receive a message; on this occasion the Mameluke is elsewhere, but two servants ride on the rear box. When Napoleon was *en route* messengers had to report to the Grand Equerry, who in his turn handed the message to the Emperor. (Collection Alfred & Roland Umhey, Germany)**

## 1815: The road to the frontier

Now, at daybreak on Monday 12 June 1815, Napoleon left Paris for Laon. The first destination was Avesnes, and relays of couriers and remounts were organized along the Paris–Avesnes road, with principal posts further on at Soissons and Laon. The latter, a fortified town, would become the administrative pivot between France and the Army of the North. Most of the Civil and Military Households, the Imperial

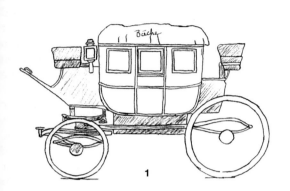

Sketch elevations of types of Household coach:
(1) Coach used by secretaries, for Cabinet papers, by Wardrobe staff and other servants
(2) Coach for members of the Household and officers
(3) Coach used by members of the Cabinet, and the Emperor's kitchen and bedchamber staff – *'la Bouche et la Chambre'*
(4) A 'Briska'
(5) The Emperor's coach.

(All courtesy Musée de l'Empéri/former Brunon Collection, Salon de Provence, France)

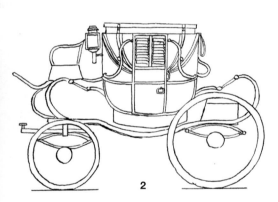

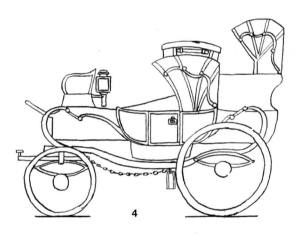

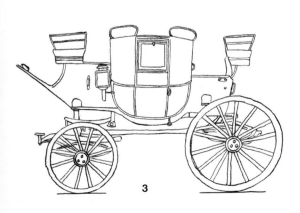

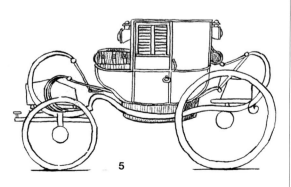

The security of the Emperor's train was assured by the *Gendarmes d'élite* of the Imperial Guard. This officer wears the popular *surtout,* a plain dark blue single-breasted jacket, with a black neck stock for campaign dress – at other times it was white. As an officer he wears the Imperial Guard aiguillettes on his right shoulder. (Courtesy Musée de l'Empéri/former Brunon Collection, Salon de Provence, France)

Headquarters and the Emperor's Cabinet, guarded by a detachment of Elite Gendarmes of the Imperial Guard, were already on the road or waiting for him to join them. Based on a document from 1812, and knowing that arrangements for the 1815 campaign were based on the 1812 decree, we may suggest that the organization was as follows:

The ten *brigades de chevaux de selle* (reserve saddle horses) were each accompanied by a corporal and two gendarmes. The six 'canteen' teams were each guarded by an NCO or corporal and two gendarmes. The four tents had four gendarmes, and two more guarded two of the Emperor's campaign beds and other items in the same *service.* The 'canteens' of the bureau were allotted two corporals and two gendarmes; two 'Briskas' loaded with food were each guarded by another gendarme. Each relay station was manned by two corporals and 20 gendarmes under an NCO.

The *Équipage d'expédition* (field train) consisted of an officer, two NCOs, two corporals and eight gendarmes, of which one officer guarded the Emperor's coach and an NCO and two men that of his Cabinet. For the General Headquarters provisions an officer, an NCO and 12 gendarmes were needed; and an officer, an NCO, two corporals and eight men guarded the heavy baggage train. The military post office was accompanied by an NCO and two gendarmes; the Headquarters horse relays for staff officers and couriers were guarded by an officer, an NCO and six gendarmes, and the ten remount relays along the road by two officers and two gendarmes each. All other relay stations were manned by Gendarmes of the Line, but under the command of an officer of the Elite Gendarmes. A final duty of the Gendarmes of the Guard was to accompany the reserve provisions for the Headquarters, with an officer, two corporals and eight men. In general the overall task of the Elite Gendarmes was to escort the Emperor's convoys during the march and to help the household staff in keeping order and discipline.

Of the vehicles that left Paris together with the Emperor only Household supply wagon No. 420 and its personnel would remain at Laon; the other 13 carriages would remain with the army. The *dormeuse* No. 389 and *landau* No. 301 would follow the Emperor closely; those carriages assigned to stay with the army travelled with the Imperial Headquarters; and the rest, together with the wagons of the Household would stay with the rearguard *Gros équipages.*[5]

To prepare the Emperor's quarters and those of his immediate suite, several carriages would leave at least a day before Napoleon himself. They would take some senior Military and Civil Household officers, a *fourrier du Palais* (palace quartermaster) and a multitude of valets and kitchen staff, who would prepare the Emperor's first quarters on the

5 On 29 January 1812 the Emperor had had for his own use and that of his immediate staff 1,485 wagons and 73 carriages. The former were of three different models; Napoleon wanted these changed for a single model with wooden-covered body, with the weight of the load painted on each.

road towards the army. A second similar party would follow the Emperor, rotating so that one was always preparing quarters ahead while the other served with the Emperor and cleaned up after he had left. Each of the two detachments carried a complete set of his necessities, such as the famous dressing case. One of the vehicles was a kitchen wagon carrying a portable oven, pots and pans and a supply of wine.

The sound of the iron-rimmed wheels on the cobbles and the sight of the imperial coat of arms painted on the doors attracted the attention of civilians along the route. Some 18 miles *(lieues)* from Paris, at Villers Cotteret, one of the spectators was Alexandre Dumas the Elder, who recalled in his memoirs:

'At 6 o'clock in the morning, I was waiting at the end of Rue de Largny with other fit inhabitants – that is to say, one had to be able to run as fast as the imperial carriages. To get a glimpse of Napoleon one needed to try to be at one of the relays. I knew this too well and, seeing the dust of the approaching horses a quarter of a mile from where I was, I started running towards the relay. The closer I came the louder the thundering of the approaching carriages sounded. At the relay, I turned round and saw the three carriages arriving like a whirlwind, pulled by sweaty horses and driven by postilions in full dress and powdered hair. Everyone ran towards the Emperor's coach; of course, I arrived among the first. The Emperor, dressed in his green uniform bearing the star of the Legion of Honour, was sitting at the far end in a corner. At his left

A trooper of the *Gendarmerie d'élite* of the Guard in full dress. These tall men, always mounted on black horses, wore dark blue uniforms with the collar in the same colour, red lapels and turn-backs; the smallclothes are ochre/buff, and rankers wore the white aiguillettes on the left shoulder. They were very recognizable by their bearskin bonnet, which had a leather front peak. The shabraque and holster covers are dark blue laced with white, with a red outer trim. The Elite Gendarmes not only escorted the different elements of the Emperor's train, but also helped with clearing the ground for his field quarters and erecting his tents. (Courtesy Musée de l'Empéri/former Brunon Collection, Salon de Provence, France)

sat his brother Jérôme and opposite him his ADC General Letort. The Emperor raised his pale head, looked around and asked:
"Where are we?"
"At Villers Cotteret, Sire", someone replied.
"So – six *lieues* from Soissons?"
"Yes, Sire, six miles from Soissons".
"Hurry up", he replied, lowering his head towards his chest.

'In the meantime the horses were changed and postilions replaced. With shouts of "Vive l'Empereur!" and the whips cracking, the coach left at speed and disappeared down the Rue de Soissons. The impressive spectacle was over.'

The *dormeuse* took the road towards Soissons, where the Emperor had a quick meal, visited the town and inspected the garrison before leaving for Laon via Chavignon, Urcel, Etouvelles, Chiny and Semilly, and arriving at about noon. Even after the previous disasters of invasion, Russian occupation, and the sacking and burning of whole quarters of the city, the citizens of Laon received him with enthusiasm. Artillery salutes, the ringing of church bells and singing filled the air, and the city notables presented themselves to offer their loyalty. Accompanied by National Guards instead of his Mounted Chasseurs, Napoleon inspected the town's fortifications, before returning at around 7pm to the Prefecture where his 'palace' was installed. In the evening the whole city was illuminated in his honour.

**Field quarters**
During Napoleon's campaigns throughout Europe, houses, castles, inns, barns and even huts temporarily became known as 'the Imperial Palace'. When they saw the miserable shacks where the Emperor was sometimes obliged to shelter the officers of his suite found this term ridiculous. Castellane recalled that it was sometimes difficult not to laugh at the seriousness with which the Emperor announced, 'I'm going to the Palace'.

At more than one place, his tent was erected in the middle of his army; but any bivouac fire might offer the Emperor hospitality. Sometimes Napoleon mentions his nomadic and dangerous life in his letters to Josephine: 'I'm a little bit tired, and bivouacked eight days in the open air, and chilly nights… We have mud knee-high… We are in a terrible village… I received your letter in a terrible barn with mud everywhere, drafty and with straw for a bed… I'm very tired, for several days now we have been bivouacking…'

In 1805, near Ulm, he found his quarters in a farmhouse room where a wounded drummer boy had taken shelter. The Emperor's servants wanted to get him out, but the young boy refused, and defended himself as best he could. Napoleon ordered them to leave him where he was, and the two slept in the same room. On 29 December that year, in the village of Kandia, the Headquarters occupied several buildings which were so bad that the Emperor chose to sleep in his carriage. At Austerlitz, during the night of 30 November/1 December, a woodcutter's hut on top of the Schlapanitz hill offered him some shelter, with straw to rest on and a fire in the middle of the floor; Napoleon would recall this as the 'most beautiful night of his life'.

On the evening after the battle of Jena in 1806 an inn was chosen for his quarters, but before he could move into it the Emperor had fallen asleep on the ground on top of his maps. His Grenadiers noticed this and, on a sign from Marshal Lefebvre, they formed a square around him to protect his rest, on the ground where they had just defeated the Prussians.

On 22 April 1809, after his victory at Eckmühl, the Emperor bedded down in the castle of Alt-Egglofsheim, but was forced to leave it during the night when a fire broke out, and spent the rest of the night sleeping in a garden in the nearby village. He spent the night before the battle of Wagram within range of the enemy, sleeping in the open air in the midst of his Guard, covered only by his coat; on the evening after his victory his tents were erected on the battlefield.

The same happened in Russia on 25 July 1812, about 3 miles from Ostrovno. At Vitebsk, Napoleon had the houses in front of the Headquarters demolished to make space for a parade square. On 16 and 17 August the Emperor bivouacked in front of Smolensk; on 7 September he had his tents pitched on the Borodino battlefield, not far from where the first redoubt had been taken. On 24 October, at Ghorodnia, a weaver's wooden hut, dilapidated and filthy, served as 'the Palace'. Another, at Zanivski, had two rooms – one for the Emperor and the other for his suite, who slept all mixed and packed together like cattle in a byre. Even worse was a shelter on 1 December at Staïki, which they christened Misérovo ('misery town'). There the Emperor and Berthier each had a small niche measuring 7 to 8 square feet, while the suite occupied one other room; it snowed so hard that members of the staff and Households all came looking for shelter. They became so packed that each man had to sleep on his side; Caulaincourt recalled that 'We were so close to each other that if a needle had fallen, it wouldn't have reached the floor'.

Around the 'Palace' all the other officers and servants in the Emperor's immediate service normally gathered. Nearby would be found the

Napoleon on the eve of Austerlitz, 1805, by Lejeune. When on campaign – or at least, his earlier ones – the Emperor accepted whatever overnight quarters were available. Here we see Roustam spreading out a fur on a layer of straw to make the simplest of beds, while servants in imperial livery unload the coach and gather firewood. (Collection Alfred & Roland Umhey, Germany)

household of Marshal Berthier, who was always followed by a huge train of carriages, supply wagons, equipment, horses and servants; the staffs and servants of Secretary of State Maret, Intendant General Daru, the Treasurer, the Inspector Generals of the Artillery and Engineers, the Colonel-Generals of the Imperial Guard, and sometimes even the entourage of the Minister of Foreign Affairs. The security of this enormous gathering of officers and functionaries was ensured by Marshal Berthier's personal guard battalion, the Swiss troops of the Bataillon de Neuchâtel. The final human rampart around this entire moving palace was provided by the Imperial Guard, imposing and arrogant, who insisted on their privileges over all Line troops or servants, sometimes to the extent of causing turmoil in the imperial camp.

Life at Imperial Headquarters was full of unexpected accidents, since despite the planning many things had to be improvised at short notice and everyone had to be ready to move off at the double. Horses were kept saddled; the boxes were arranged in line so that they were easy to pack, fasten and load on the wagons even in the dark. The wagons were parked in the order of their places on the march.

### The tented camp

When they fought a battle that lasted until nightfall the imperial tents were set up on the battlefield itself. With cannon still roaring in the background, and the sky lit by fires, men started clearing corpses, wounded, wrecked limbers and wagons, cannon balls, and all manner of human and material debris from the spot where the camp was to be pitched. The Imperial Guard formed a square around the site, while mules brought in the striped blue-and-white tent canvases, poles, and camp furniture all packed in large leather bags. Officers shouted orders as the valets of the Civil Household scurried about unpacking in the darkness: the tents had to be pitched and ready in just 30 minutes.

On occasion, hastily setting up camp by night in the middle of a battlefield could produce surprises.

ometimes the enemy regained their strength and pushed forward again even while the camp was being pitched; this happened at Wagram in 1809, when the tents had to be folded up hastily and send back to the rear again. Baron Fain, Napoleon's secretary, recalled that on one occasion, after waiting longer than usual for the arrival of the tents, everyone was so tired that as soon as they were finally pitched the Emperor's entourage simply turned in and fell asleep wherever they could find a suitable space under canvas. In the morning Fain awoke to the horrible discovery that he had used a fresh corpse as a pillow instead of the usual portemanteau.

Such inconveniences might also be encountered when the 'Palace' was improvised in buildings close to a battlefield, where the human cost of Napoleon's career might be tactlessly obvious. Once, somewhere in Germany, the Emperor's quarters had to be prepared in a peasant shed that had already been used by the surgeons; first it had to be cleared of a pile of amputated limbs, and the floor and table scrubbed clean of bloodstains. During the Polish campaign, at Nazielk, Napoleon had to wait outside his new quarters while his valets carried out two corpses wrapped in straw. Again, in 1814 at Haute-Epine, the two rooms selected for the Emperor proved to be piled with corpses, and Ségur recalled in his memoirs that the servants had to work in such haste that they simply pitched the bodies out of the windows.

## 1815: Lodgings

For the Waterloo campaign tents were not used, and the 'Palace' varied between a small manorhouse and a humble farm, chosen by Lodgings Marshal de Guerchy and Palace Quartermaster Baillon, who were responsible for clearing, cleaning and preparing Napoleon's quarters.

On 13 June, at 3am, the Emperor's immediate entourage gathered at the Prefecture in Laon, and at 4.30am he and his suite mounted their

The Emperor took a large selection of books with him on campaign, specially bound so as to fit into his mahogany travelling bookcases. These had three drawers, each with three long compartments, secured with two doors at the front. (Collection du Musée National du Château de Malmaison, France)

carriages for Vervins. There, alerted by the passing of the first carriage of the train, an extremely nervous mayor stood waiting for hours to receive the Emperor, nervously rehearsing a suitable speech. When Napoleon's carriage arrived the window was lowered and the Emperor asked the mayor, 'How far are we are from Avesnes?'. 'Eight miles, Sire'. Those three words were all the mayor had time to utter before the whip cracked and the coaches drove off at speed towards Etroengt, where the entourage stopped for a hasty meal.

*   *   *

When travelling by carriage the Emperor spent most of the time tucked away in a corner, reading or looking out at the passing landscape while his companion – usually the Major-General, Grand

*Fourriers du Palais*, 'palace quartermasters', had imperial green uniforms like most members of the Household; here we see those worn in about 1806–08. (Left) is mounted undress uniform with heavy cavalry boots – plain green coat with silver embroidery, and white smallclothes; (right) is the full dress uniform with crimson collar and cuffs. (Collection Paul Meganck, Brussels)

Marshal of the Palace, Grand Equerry, or one of his marshals or ADCs – worked next to him. The Emperor worked his way through his correspondence, consulting his *carnets* of intelligence data, making decisions and ordering troop movements. The Major-General took notes, had them copied and sent off as soon as possible at the first relay station, whether by day or night.

One of Napoleon's favourite occupations on his long journeys was reading. During his reign he ordered from his librarian a collection of books with specially printed condensed texts, so that many would fit into his portable mahogany bookcases. But when a book did not satisfy him it was simply thrown out of the carriage window (to become a highly prized souvenir for those who followed the Emperor – they would jump from their horses in order to grab it first). The same happened to letters or reports, but these were ripped into pieces before being discarded along the muddy roads.

When a messenger arrived then the Grand Marshal or Grand Equerry dismounted to receive the message and to take it to the Emperor; within moments the empty envelopes would come flying out of the carriage windows.

\*     \*     \*

Early in the morning of 13 June 1815 the imperial party arrived in Avesnes. Several hours earlier the duty palace quartermaster had entered the sub-prefecture building. This official enjoyed the prestige of his position; dressed in his imperial green and silver uniform, and ranking as a lieutenant, he and the Palace Lodgings Marshal always arrived first and immediately started organizing the Emperor's quarters. The quartermaster (*fourrier*) looked after cleaning and tidying up the rooms, furnishing them and bringing in all the necessary provisions and

**From 1808 the *fourriers du Palais* started wearing a more military style of uniform, though retaining the green, red facings, and silver lace – see also the portraits of Pierre Baillon on page 53. The holster covers are in black bearskin; the round-cornered shabraque is dark green edged with silver. (Collection Paul Meganck, Brussels)**

equipment. The *maréchal des logis* was responsible fo[r] allocating quarters for the different staffs; once h[e] had selected them he procured a list of name[s] and addresses and hung it on the mo[st] important house in the village. When th[e] Emperor's lodgings were not established i[n] the departmental prefect's house, th[e] choice fell upon the most comfortab[le] building available.

As soon as the first Househol[d] officers and valets arrived word woul[d] spread like wildfire, bringing the mayo[r] the local priest and the neighbours t[o] the new 'Palace'. Suddenly, without an[y] warning, a dusty green coach embellishe[d] with the imperial coat of arms would ha[lt] in front of the chosen house. The Emper[or] would step down and, guided by the equer[ry] or duty ADC, enter the building without dela[y] climbing to his three-room quarters on the fir[st] floor, he would immediately begin pacing up an[d] down while dictating orders and letters. Below stairs th[e] cooks, already at work, would ask for the keys of the box[es] containing provisions, cutlery and plates, as well those of the 'win[e] cellar'. Outside, the pages Gudin and Cambacérès, plus some Mounte[d] Chasseurs, would try to keep the curious citizens at bay as they gawpe[d] at Ali's expensive oriental costume.[6]

When the Emperor was staying in a town or village he woul[d] sometimes make the time to listen and talk to the local magistrates. The[y] might wait for hours for an opportunity to pronounce their loyalty, on[ly] to be told to go home since the Emperor was too busy working. Whe[n] he did take the time to see them he first had to endure a speech o[f] welcome. These were often bought in Paris ready-written, proclaimin[g] the Emperor's glory and might at tedious and unoriginal length. H[e] tended to respond by simply turning away, or suddenly interrupting th[e] nervous orator with unexpected questions about the cost of living, th[e] economy, local factories, and so forth.

If he had the time, Napoleon would normally ride out early in th[e] morning to inspect the locality and any military installations lik[e] fortifications or barracks. The rest of the day he would spend working a[s] usual. Sometimes, late at night, he would call for his Mameluke to brin[g] coffee (which was always kept ready at hand). For the night, a page an[d] the duty ADC looked for a spot close to the Emperor's room where the[y] could lie down, and the Mameluke would sleep in front of the Emperor['s] door. Outside, horses were always kept saddled and bridled, ready at [a] moment's notice.

**General Bacler d'Albe, the engineer who headed the Emperor's topographical office with great skill until the 1813 German campaign. Thereafter, exhausted by his campaigns, he was named director of the *Dépôt de la Guerre* (the staff documentation branch), taking over from Gen Sanson, who had been taken prisoner in Russia. Bacler d'Albe was ably replaced by his deputy Col Atthalin and, for the Hundred Days, by Gen Simon Bernard. (Ann S.K.Brown Collection, Providence, USA)**

6  Charles Gabriel César Gudin served as a page from 15 June 1812, when he was 14; he was the son of Gen Cou[nt] de la Sablonnière, mortally wounded at Valutina during the Russian campaign. Dismissed after the First Abdicatio[n,] he entered the Wagram Company of the Royal Household's Gardes du Corps, returning to duty as a page upo[n] Napoleon's return. It was usual for the First Page to receive a cavalry commission; Gudin was commissioned lie[u-]tenant in the 3rd Hussars only on 17 June 1815, and for various reasons could not join his regiment, following th[e] Emperor back towards Paris. In later life he rose to general of division in 1852, married the daughter of Marsh[al] Mortier, and died in 1874.
The other page, Jean-Jacques Cambacérès, was a nephew of the Prince Arch-Chancellor of the Empire. Mad[e] prisoner at Waterloo, he later became Grand Master of Ceremonies under Napoleon III.

* * *

By 13 June, Napoleon knew exactly what forces were at his disposal. All the available information was placed before him and, reading maps marked with the usual multi-coloured pins, he dictated orders and messages. He also drafted his famous proclamation: *'Soldiers! Today is the anniversary of Marengo and Friedland... Victory will be ours... For all Frenchmen the time has come to conquer or to perish...'* Once the text was ready it was taken to the printer in the main square, who had to work throughout the night so that the proclamation could be distributed to the regiments before they crossed the French-Belgian border. In the late afternoon of the 13th the Emperor toured Avesnes and its fortifications, which dated from Vauban's time.

The next day, Wednesday 14 June, he dealt with state papers before travelling to Beaumont, where he installed himself in the house of Count de Riquet. The 1st Foot Grenadiers of the Guard were on duty. General officers and messengers were arriving, but the first to be received was the *maîtresse des Postes* (female postmaster), who was responsible for the communications between Mons and Chimay via Beaumont. Napoleon received her courteously, and questioned her about the roads leading into Belgium, especially those towards Charleroi.

Beaumont was packed with troops and it was difficult to find quarters. Marshal Ney, arriving at 10pm, could not find suitable lodgings, but

Once Napoleon halted and entered his campaign quarters or tented camp, the chief topographical engineer (Bacler d'Albe, Atthalin, or Bernard) would be the first to be consulted. This officer would update a map of the region with multi-coloured metal pins to indicate the different units, allied and enemy. The examples displayed here show scarlet-headed pins for French commands in the foreground; diagonal blue/white/red flags bear the commander's name/title in black – e.g. 'Vandamme' on the white stripe, and 'Oudinot/Regg' on the white/red areas for Marshal Oudinot/Duc de Reggio, etc. Russian commands have dark brown-headed pins with light green/white/green flags. (Courtesy Musée de l'Empéri/ former Brunon Collection, Salon de Provence, France)

Intendant General Daru gave up his own room to the marshal. Ney tried to see the Emperor, but was refused: Napoleon was working out and dictating the army's marching orders, and only messengers were allowed access to him. During the night a thunderstorm raged over the region and flooded the bivouacs. More than one officer worried about the conditions of the roads on which the army had to march.

On 10 June the nominal roll of the Imperial Headquarters staff consisted of the following 53 officers:

*ADCs to the Emperor:* Gens Lebrun, Drouot, Corbineau, Flahaut, Dejean & de Labédoyère, Col Bernard
*First Orderly Officer:* Col Gourgaud

*Major-General:* Marshal Soult
*Chief of Staff:* LtGen Count Bailly de Monthion
*Responsible for prisoners of war:* Maréchal de camp Baron Dentzel
*Adjutants-commandants:* Baron Michal, Baron Stoffel, Babut, d'Hincour & Petiet
*Superior officers serving with the Staff:* Maréchaux de camp Lebel, Baron Gressot & Baron Couture; Cols Count Gramont, Raoul, Count Forbin de Janson, Hugo, Zenowicz & Duzaire; Majors Dessaix & Tessier de Marguerittes; Chefs de bn Dalbenas, Girard, Rollin, Grondal Laplace, Lefebure, Gentet, Waleski, Desmarquets de Ciré Bernard, Arnaud, Favelas, Fourchy, Hirne & Deschamps Capts Clavet Gaubert, Descrivieux, de Joly, Dulnas de Saint Léon, Noailles, Coignet (famous for his 'Cahiers or memoirs), Baudisson, Guettard, Favier & Ramorino; and Sub-lieutenant Garda.

**Imperial Household pages had a relatively plain single-breasted campaign dress; however, Gros represented this page wearing a coat with gold buttonhole loops in conjunction with campaign riding boots and ochre leather breeches. Sources also show the Emperor's valets represented in this type of dress. (Collection Paul Meganck, Brussels)**

As in the past, the staff of the Major-General the administration of Intendant General Daru Treasurer General Baron Peyrusse, the commanders of artillery and engineers Count Ruty and Baron Rogniat and their respective staffs all found their quarters close to the 'Palace' The Headquarters topographical office was commanded by Col Bonne, and the Gendarmerie by Grand Provost LtGen Radet; the *Inspecteur aux revues* was Lambert. The Belgian-born Col J.L.Crabbé (1768–1816) was responsible for keeping order and protection of the Imperial Headquarters which was guarded each day by a different Old Guard infantry battalion in rotation. (On 18 June, Crabbé would be sent to serve with Marshal Ney; after charging with him at Waterloo he left the battlefield wounded.)

### 1815: Soult as Major-General of the Army of the North

An old soldier is said to have written to the Emperor in 1815, 'Don't use the marshals'. In 1814 many veterans, officers and rankers alike, had been shocked witnesses to the changeable loyalty of marshals who accommodated themselves to the service of the restored Bourbon king.

After regaining his throne, the Emperor reorganized his army with the help of Marshal Davout, who now acted as Minister of War. Marshal Mortier would command the Cavalry of the Guard, but he would be bedridden by illness before the campaign started. Marshal Grouchy was newly appointed, and Marshal Ney would only be called upon as a last resort to replace Mortier.

The other marshal Napoleon employed was Soult, who in 1813 had briefly replaced Berthier as Major-General. Prior to this brief appointment, Soult had served as a divisional staff officer during the Revolutionary Wars; and in Spain he had been commissioned Major-General to King Joseph, though the latter commission was more a commander-in-chief's post than a real staff job. Initially Napoleon appointed Gen Bailly de Monthion as chief of staff to the Army of the North; in this long-time aide to Berthier the Emperor knew that he had an experienced officer in this critical post. However, having fought his previous campaigns with a marshal as Major-General, Napoleon – who perhaps still hoped for the return of Marshal Berthier – believed that he had to appoint another senior marshal to the post in order to impose his will upon the commanding generals.

Soult accepted the appointment on 9 May 1815, but questions about both his loyalty and his suitability for the post arose immediately, due to Soult's conduct since the First Abdication. As Minister of War from 4 December 1814 until 11 March 1815 he had made many enemies among veteran officers. General Vandamme would not even shake hands with him, refusing to accept orders from Soult until he was ordered to obey by the Emperor himself, and many other officers would not salute him. This did not deter the Emperor, who believed that his own prestige was sufficient to impose his choice upon them.

Napoleon was a great strategist, but he was unable to make forecasts without accurate intelligence reports on the enemy's positions and intentions. He was gifted with very keen observation, and his deductions were rapid and logical, although sometimes exaggerated by his imagination. When he was properly briefed, with even the barest of accurate information, his decisions were instantaneous; but when he did not know what was going on he would walk about, hands behind his back, or go to sleep while awaiting information.

To help him plan his earlier campaigns, the Emperor surrounded himself with eager young officers who clearly understood his intentions. From 1812 onwards this changed, due to casualties, bigger armies, and fewer experienced staff officers. The Emperor still dictated his orders in the same style, and Berthier was well able to read his intentions and to add any necessary clarifications to the instructions which went out to the

ADCs to a general were usually young officers either of noble birth, or who had distinguished themselves by their bravery on several occasions. This young blade shows the elegance typical of his class; note the high white shirt collar and fashionable haircut. On his left arm can just be seen the regulation brassard: white and gold for ADC to a marshal, red and gold for ADC to a *général de division*, and sky-blue and gold for ADC to a *général de brigade*. (Courtesy Musée de l'Empéri/former Brunon Collection, Salon de Provence, France)

line commanders. Bailly de Monthion had the same ability; but Soult lacked it, and his selection for an office that he had never before filled was to have disastrous consequences – the role of Major-General was not something one could improvise. Moreover, the superceded Bailly de Monthion could not work with Soult; and perhaps one also needs to consider the personal relationship between Napoleon and Soult. In Spain, Soult had always exercised an independent command backed by an experienced staff corps. Now, serving as Major-General under the Emperor's eye, he was expected to be a second Berthier, and was bound to fall short of that uniquely talented administrator's encyclopaedic knowledge of every detail of staff routine.

While Soult failed as Major-General, one must not forget that it was he and his staff who prepared the campaign; and that when Napoleon lost all hope and all control of the situation after Waterloo, Soult

*(text continued on page 42)*

An ADC in regulation dark blue uniform with sky-blue collar, cuffs and false turnbacks, black hat with sky-blue plume, and light cavalry saddlery and harness. During the Waterloo campaign many of Marshal Soult's despatches either failed to arrive, or were seriously delayed; on 16 June this played a part in preventing Gen d'Erlon's I Corps from reinforcing either Ney at Quatre Bras or Napoleon at Ligny. On 17–18 June – as is notorious – communications between the Emperor and Marshal Grouchy were fatally muddled, preventing the latter from intervening between Blücher's Prussians and the battlefield of Waterloo. (Author's collection)

ORDERLY OFFICERS TO THE EMPEROR; ELBA, 1814
1: Regulation full dress, mounted
2: Full dress, unmounted, summer
3: Evening dress

A

POSTILIONS OF THE IMPERIAL HOUSEHOLD & HEADQUARTERS

VALETS TO THE EMPEROR
1: Small livery; campaign dress, 1805–07
2 & 3: Full livery; campaign dress, 1804–15
4: Winter riding dress

F. Courcelle

MILITARY POSTAL SERVICE & SPECIAL COURIER
1: Inspector-in-chief, Military Postal Service, 1809–15
2: Sub-employee, Military Postal Service
3: Courier, Military Postal Service
4: 'Moustache', First Courier to the Emperor, 1804–06

P. Courcelle

POSTAL SERVICE & COURIERS
1: Imperial courier, c.1804–06
2: Army GHQ courier, c.1806–07
3: Driver, Imperial Postal Service, c.1810–12

E

ARMY GENERAL HEADQUARTERS PERSONNEL
1: Grenadier, Bataillon de Neuchâtel, 1806–12
2: Courier to the Major-General, c.1807–09
3: Guide-interpreter of the Army of Germany, 1805

F

GUIDES OF THE PRINCE OF NEUCHÂTEL
1: Officer, daily uniform, c.1807–10
2: Guide, Compagnie d'élite du GQG, c.1810–11
3: Guide, 1814

P. Courcelle

**G**

THE EMPEROR'S TENTED CAMP, RUSSIA, 1812

Plan of the tented camp of the Emperor in Russia, reconstructed after the 1812 decree on the composition of the Emperor's train, now in the Caulaincourt papers in the National Archives, Paris – see also Plate H opposite.

The Emperor's quarters consisted of three round tents (two of them lined) and one oval tent (also lined). The Grand Officers of the Household had one round and one oval tent, as did the Emperor's ADCs. His orderly officers had one round tent, and the officers of the duty units another. The secretaries had to share one with the palace lodging marshals (*maréchaux des logis du Palais*), and the palace quartermasters (*fourriers du Palais*) with the medical officers. Three teams of servants providing the most immediate personal services to the Emperor (*bouche*, table; *écuries*, stables; and *chambre*, body servants) each had one round tent; and the other servants shared two others. The kitchens occupied four oval tents.

The tents and furniture of the Imperial camp were normally transported in four wagons, one of them carrying the Emperor's four tents. Not shown here are four smaller square tents, each with an external marquee; these were alternatives for the *Service léger* or Light Field Service, carried by one mule each.

The dimensions of the original plan are given in *toises* – roughly, paces; the details are not to minutely exact scale.

(1) The Emperor
(2) The Grand Officers (Grand Marshal, Grand Equerry)
(3) Aides de camp
(4) Orderly officers
(5) Lodging marshals & secretaries
(6) Officers of duty units of the Guard
(7) Quartermasters & medical officers
(8) Valets
(9) Emperor's suite (*écuries*)
(10) Emperor's suite (*chambre*). Erratum: on Plate H this is wrongly shown as an oval tent – see plan for correct size & position, allowing quick access to the horse lines
(11) Emperor's suite (*bouche*)
(12) Kitchens
(13) *Vivandiers* – varying numbers, depending on the number of troops
(14) Main guard
(15) Guard posts
(16) Horses – duty outriders (*piquers*) & duty officers
(17) Horses – varying numbers of picket lines
(18) Vehicles & baggage
(19) Duty squadron of Guard cavalry
(20) Duty battalion of Guard infantry

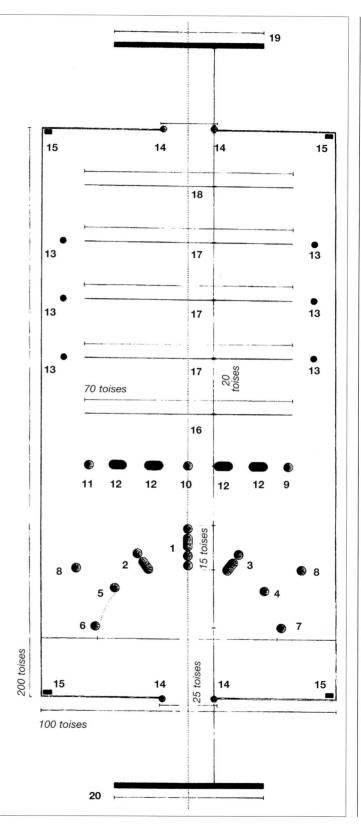

became once again the effective commander-in-chief, concentrating the army in France where, with Davout, he would organize the last defences of the Empire.

## 1815: Meals en route

The Emperor and his staff left Beaumont at 3.30am on Thursday 15 June. Surrounded by his escort of Mounted Chasseurs and followed by the duty squadrons, he rode to Thuillies and Marbaix-la-Tour. Normally, the officers following the Emperor dared not pass the imperial escort; only superior officers had the right to come any closer to the Emperor. Day and night and facing every risk, these staff and Household officers followed the Emperor at full trot. Only the two leading Chasseurs and the two orderly officers who rode in front of the carriage had any room to ride the narrow roads in safety. All the others risked falling and breaking limbs (or neck) as they rode at full speed, crammed together and half-blinded by darkness, fog or dust, each one – orderly officer or 'Chasseur of the Portfolio', groom or page – convinced of his own importance and his duty to follow the Emperor as closely as possible.

When Napoleon was actually with his armies he would usually travel on horseback. He was a mediocre horseman, but one who could ride for hours, with his right arm hanging down and his left hand holding the reins – though in fact it was his horse that controlled him. He would suddenly decide that he had to be on the move, and would give the order to mount before his suite and escorts were ready; the Emperor and three or four officers would already have galloped 200–300 yards before the rest could catch up and take their places. Sometimes they would ride in pensive silence; sometimes Napoleon took the lead, and his entourage could chat as they rode. On arriving before any obstacle that might conceal danger, such as a small bridge or a ditch, the Grand Equerry would take the lead and cross it first.

One day, riding on a difficult muddy road, a Mounted Chasseur who fell from his horse was rebuked by the Emperor as a bungler. Moments later the Emperor in his turn fell from the saddle, at which the trooper was heard to remark that 'It seems I'm not the only bungler today!'

Shortly before 7am on 15 June, after riding for more than 3½ hours already, Napoleon halted near Les Quatre Chemins. Sitting on a chair and sucking a few fresh raw eggs, he warmed himself near a fire. When on campaign, convenient places for a brief halt to eat were normally pointed out by the Grand Marshal or the Grand Equerry; but there was no firm schedule, since halts and departures, planned routes and prepared quarters could change from one moment to the next. Napoleon's timetable and itinerary depended on the arrival of couriers and reports of the latest developments. Sometimes he stopped in a field, dismounted and sat under a tree, calling for something to eat. Roustam and the valets would take him provisions stored in the Emperor's coach or in the mess canteens carried by different members of his suite. During his 15-year reign Napoleon always drank Chambertin wine diluted with water, which he thought was good for his health. Fine Chambertin was consequently carried for him throughout the whole of Europe, from Germany to Spain and even to Moscow. (Apart from the private provisions of the superior officers, Chambertin was the only wine carried for the Headquarters on campaign, but ordinary table wine was normally acquired on the spot.)

Rear view of a Mounted Chasseur of the Guard wearing winter campaign dress including the short, round, dark green cloak; note the plain black sabretache, and green overalls heavily reinforced with black leather on the inside legs, and with a red-striped outer seam buttoned down. (Collection Paul Meganck, Brussels)

When following the army, as soon as the Grand Marshal indicated a place where a meal should be prepared, the *maître d'hôtel*, two cooks and a *garçon de fourneau* ('stove boy') would swiftly begin work.[7] The Emperor was served by *Maître-contrôleur* Pfister until 1809, when that unfortunate servant fell insane, and was replaced by Colin. Though of sober habits, the Emperor might call for food at any time of the day or night, and due to these irregular hours the kitchen service had to see to it that there were always warm meals ready in silver casseroles – a promptness that earned his praise on several occasions. Napoleon's favourites were chicken in several styles, ham, partridges, salads of green

---

7 The cooks were Dunan, Léonard, Rouff & Gerrard; the sons of the wine merchants Soupé and Pierrugues also rotated with the kitchen staff.

beans, lentils and potatoes. At breakfast the Emperor usually ate alone, on a round mahogany stand without a cloth; this snack normally detained him for only eight to ten minutes.

At each of these halts other vehicles would bring in more members of his staff and entourage. A fire was lit to heat coffee, and the rest of the Emperor's suite joined him for a quick bite to eat. In less than half an hour everything was finished and the carriages took the road again. When the meal was prepared in a town or a roadside house the kitchen staff would use what could be obtained on the spot, and on departure everything was paid for in cash by the Paymaster General. Gifts were given to the proprietors of the house, and everything not necessary was left behind for their servants. While the service of the Grand Equerry was always under the strictest control, the kitchen department was more

LEFT AND OPPOSITE
**The difference between Bonaparte's uniform styles during the Revolution and Consulate, and the Empire, was significant – he was a master of the manipulated public image. Early in his career Napoleon wore elaborate laced waist belts and hats trimmed with gold braid. When he was with his armies during the campaigns of the Empire he made a point of dressing in simple, almost austere uniform, in contrast to the showy splendour of his marshals and senior generals. (Collection Paul Meganck, Brussels)**

flexibly supervised when on campaign. At all levels of its hierarchy certain benefits might stick to their fingers, or to those of the suppliers of provisions or owners of billets. However, from the Austrian campaign of 1809 onwards a new office was created to keep control of all expenses.

Typically, the Emperor sometimes decided that it was too early for lunch after all, or that he wanted to have more time in the field, and ordered his staff to move on without preparing food. Even as his extended entourage were riding up, grateful at the prospect of a halt and a meal, he would suddenly call for his carriage or horse, creating a chain reaction. Everyone immediately had to set off as fast as possible in order to regain their place in the column, leaving the cooks and servants behind to pack everything up and try to follow the Emperor to the next possible halt.

When the 'Palace' was installed for a longer period on the same spot, crystal and silver- or gold-plated tableware came out, and dinner was provided for the staff, Households and visiting officers. The Emperor normally ate with Berthier, or Murat when the latter was present. Three other tables were set near to Napoleon's. One was for Caulaincourt,

Prefect of the Palace Bausset, marshals visiting the HQ, foreign generals, Napoleon's ADCs, Gen Guyot commanding the duty squadrons, Chamberlain de Turenne, and two equerries. The second was for Napoleon's orderly officers, the *petits aides-de-camp*, the guard duty officers and those of the Gendarmerie d'Elite, the Civil Household, surgeons, Treasurer Peyrusse, and the Imperial Pages. The third was for the Cabinet staff, who ate after the Emperor had been served

Sometimes the Emperor walked around the tables, stopping and observing, but the guests were to carry on eating as if he were not there. ADCs of the marshals and corps commanders, who brought messages or were on duty near the Emperor, also ate with the other staff officers. By this means the Household and duty officers soon knew what was going on at all points of the front. Messengers, couriers or officers returning from a mission had unlimited access, and the Emperor would listen to them without interrupting his meal.

# 1815: ACROSS THE FRONTIER

With his troops crossing the Belgian frontier northwards, Napoleon's intentions became clear: to smash past Charleroi with 122,000 men and 374 guns, crossing the River Sambre at that point. Depending upon Allied reactions, he might be able to take Blücher's Prussian Army of the Lower Rhine by surprise, and to defeat them before they could effect any junction with Wellington's British, Dutch-Belgian and Hanoverian army further to the west. But the planned invasion of Belgium had started with the first signs of failing staff work: Gen Vandamme could not be found by Soult's messenger, who got lost and fell from his horse, breaking a leg. It was calculated that the different corps had to march off at half-hourly intervals; the delay of Vandamme's III Corps triggered confusion, as different columns arrived together to jam the bridges at Charleroi.

The marching orders were too wordy and cluttered with detail, creating misunderstandings; in Berthier's time, important orders would have been expressed succinctly – and sent in duplicate, triplicate or even quadruplicate. Soult's personal staff were not up to the job; his ADCs needed more time to deliver their messages than before, and five times out of six they got lost, or arrived too late for their confusingly drafted despatches to achieve the desired effect. Further inefficiencies of staff work soon became apparent; and some generals started to notice that the Emperor was not the same man he had been even a year earlier.

\* \* \*

At Jamioulx the Emperor's suite halted in a field near the vicarage; a table and a few chairs were sufficient for their needs. Messengers and ADCs came and went; orders were given for the different corps marching towards Charleroi, but once again the orders were unclear, referring to villages and roads that did not in fact exist. Thinking the job done, the Emperor took the road towards Charleroi via Marcinelle, where he drank a beer. At noon on 15 June, Napoleon entered Charleroi and First Chamberlain de Turenne guided him to his 'Palace', the château of an ironmaster named Puissant. By the time he dismounted and thanked the owner the inner courtyard was already aswarm with activity. While the Civil Household worked to prepare the château, Napoleon's halt lasted only a few minutes before he stepped into his carriage, and his entourage mounted hastily to take their places. They rode through the city and reconnoitred the suburbs; passing out through the North Gate, they stopped at the next crossroads at the Cabaret de la Belle Vue near the Brussels and Fleurus roads. There the Emperor asked for a chair; sitting astride it, as usual, he fell asleep, unwoken even by the cheers of passing regiments. (Since then the inn has also been called the 'Auberge de la Somnolence'.)

At 2pm, First Orderly Officer Gen Gourgaud returned from Lodelinsart with the news that the Prussians were retreating north-eastwards via Gilly. An hour and a quarter later, Marshal Ney presented himself to receive the Emperor's orders. Verbally, and without later confirmation in writing, he was given command of the army's left wing (I & II Corps plus cavalry) and his instructions, upon which he left instantly for Gosselies, on the road due north towards Brussels. (Without the evidence of written orders, his exercise of command at Quatre-Bras the following day would become the subject of lively controversy.) Soon afterwards the newly created Marshal Grouchy arrived, and left around 4pm with the Emperor, heading towards Gilly. There Napoleon looked over the Prussian positions from a windmill: the enemy had formed a strong position astride the road towards Fleurus. The Emperor – again verbally and without written confirmation – gave Grouchy command of the right wing of the Army of the North (III & IV Corps plus cavalry), before returning to Charleroi. Napoleon retained personal control of the Guard and Gen Lobau's VI Corps.

At 5.30pm on the 15th, after receiving a delegation of local dignitaries and taking a light meal, Napoleon once more took the road towards Gilly, where he had expected to hear the sound of gunfire. However, when he arrived at the crossroads shortly after 6pm no action was taking place. After another examination from the top of the windmill, he crossed the creek of Lodelinsart and took up position closer to the Prussian rearguard. Impatient of the resistance that the enemy was building up, he ordered his ADC Gen Letort, commander of the Dragoons of the Imperial Guard, to take the Guard duty squadrons and 'break down that scum' (*'d'enfoncer la canaille'*). Two squares were duly swept aside, but Gen Letort was mortally wounded. By around 8pm the Prussians were in flight; the tired Emperor left the mopping up to Grouchy and returned to Charleroi.

Napoleon went straight to his room, where his valets unbuttoned his uniform and took off his boots; apparently unconcerned, he went to bed. During the night Marshal Ney reported to the Emperor and had a light meal with him, leaving around 2am on the morning of the 16th, with verbal orders which anticipated the main effort that day being on Ney's left flank, against Wellington's Allied army in the direction of

Louis, Baron Séganville (1776–1844), became an ADC to Marshal Bessières in the rank of lieutenant on 22 November 1800. Progressing steadily through the ranks, he was promoted colonel on 2 February 1808. From March 1813 – a couple of months before his marshal was killed at Rippach – he commanded line cavalry regiments. Here he is seen as ADC to Bessières, wearing his epaulettes of colonel and the aiguillettes of the Imperial Guard on a double-breasted *redingote*. (Courtesy Musée de l'Empéri/ former Brunon Collection, Salon de Provence, France)

Brussels. Napoleon returned to bed and tried to get a couple more hours' rest, though interrupted several times by arriving messengers.

\* \* \*

After his broken night the Emperor rose at 4am on 16 June, to read and listen to the reports on Allied movements. Two hours later, orders were sent out to the different corps commanders. These contained marching orders, and instructions as to the wing of the army to which each corps would be attached. General Drouot received orders to march with the Imperial Guard towards Fleurus. Messages from Grouchy had confirmed that, unexpectedly, Blücher's Prussians seemed to be drawing up in strength around Ligny. By about 8am all orders had been sent, and the Emperor left Charleroi for Fleurus two hours later. Arriving between 11am and noon, he found that the Prussians were indeed holding a number of villages along the Quatre-Bras/Sombreffe/Namur road, behind an advanced position at Ligny.

After riding along the vanguards of the French army, Napoleon dismounted near a windmill against whose walls the engineers had constructed an observation post. From this vantage point he examined the

potential battlefield of Ligny, and questioned a local guide. At around
1pm, Gen Gérard came for orders while his IV Corps were slowly
marching towards their positions east of Ligny. Descending from the
platform, the Emperor gave his generals instructions for their parts in the
L-shaped deployment of the army.

The Guard artillery opened the engagement at about 2.30pm with
their usual three-gun salvo. The battle raged furiously through the
villages, but remained indecisive, and once again orders did not arrive
when and where they were needed. General Vandamme did not receive
the order to put his III Corps under the overall command of Marshal
Grouchy, resulting in unpleasant and time-consuming argument. Ney –
of whose simultaneous battle against Wellington at Quatre-Bras off to
the west the Emperor was apparently ignorant – was supposed to send
troops eastwards to reinforce Napoleon's left flank; but if the order was
ever sent, it was not received in time. Impatiently, the Emperor took
personal command and ordered the Imperial Guard to attack.
Overwhelmed, the Prussians retreated northwards that night towards
Wavre, under command of the chief of staff Gen Gneisenau while old
Blücher recovered from his injuries.

Much time had been wasted. Himself expecting to be reinforced with Gen d'Erlon's I Corps for a major thrust towards Brussels via Quatre Bras, Marshal Ney had not committed Gen Reille's II Corps to attacking the rapidly reinforced British/Dutch-Belgian force at that crossroads until the afternoon. Confused orders and delayed communications had left Gen d'Erlon counter-marching uselessly between Ligny and Quatre Bras all day; the staff failures had cost the French decisive victory in at least one and perhaps both of these battles. Nevertheless, on the evening of 16 June the Emperor appeared to be satisfied – he seemed to have succeeded in keeping the Allied armies divided, and did not believe that the Prussians could recover. Inexplicably, he refused to allow Grouchy to mount a serious pursuit of Blücher's apparently beaten army that night.

At 11pm he returned, very tired, to Fleurus, where his quarters were set up in the Château de la Paix of Chevalier P.de Barchifontaine. The Imperial Headquarters were accommodated opposite in another manor-house, that of Baron de Zualart, and around a brick windmill close by.

*   *   *

On 17 June at 7am the Emperor had breakfast with his ADC Gen Flahaut. Leaving for Ligny in his coach, Napoleon was frustrated by its slow progress and continued on horseback; eyewitnesses were struck by his appearance of great fatigue and lethargy. He inspected the troops, who were annoyed at having to spend time cleaning their uniforms and equipment, and toured the battlefield with Grouchy – whom he still refused permission to pursue the Prussians until he had the latest reports from Ney. Again inexplicably, it was mid-morning before these arrived: Ney had been unable to seize the Quatre-Bras crossroads, and Wellington's troops were still in undisturbed possession of this strategic junction. At around 11am Napoleon finally instructed Grouchy to follow the Prussians northwards, while he and Ney's left wing advanced against Wellington, whom he no doubt hoped to outflank. Some time before mid-day Soult joined the Emperor; mounted on Désirée, and followed by Gen Colbert's Guard Lancers, Napoleon rode westwards, and at about 2pm met Ney near Quatre-Bras – where he discovered that the morning had been completely wasted.

Since May the inhabitants of the area around Waterloo and Braine l'Alleud had known that something important was pending, as Allied troops established camps and quarters in this region. On the evening of 15 June their concern that war was approaching their quiet fields had been confirmed: travellers from the direction of Charleroi reported that the Emperor had crossed the frontier. The following day the villagers of Genappe were awakened by the unmistakable music of red-coated Scottish troops marching south from Brussels towards Quatre-Bras. In the muggy heat they put out water butts for the thirsty soldiers; and as the day wore on more and more Allied units passed by, heading south towards the distant rumble of gunfire.

On 17 June the British/Dutch-Belgian force from Quatre-Bras came marching northwards again towards Mont Saint Jean and nearby Waterloo, preceded by wagons with a bloody cargo of wounded. They had successfully blocked Ney at the crossroads on the 16th; but with the reunification of his and the Emperor's troops, and incomplete information about the whereabouts or intentions of the Prussians away to the north-east, Wellington had to fall back up the road to the capital. He conducted a rapid but controlled retreat, while his rearguard cavalry and horse artillery fended off the French pursuers who belatedly followed. A massive rainstorm turned the fields into swamps; this hindered the pursuit, but did nothing for the Allied soldiers' mood, and more than one house was looted. Some Dutch-Belgian officers warned the inhabitants to shut themselves in and not to open doors to the soldiers, but most of the civilians simply fled towards safer villages in the neighbourhood.

Late in the afternoon Genappe was disturbed for a second time: over the splashing of the rain, hooves and wheels were heard on the cobblestones once again. French cavalry and guns were passing northwards at speed, towards the hamlets of Maison du Roi and La Belle Alliance. At Le Caillou farm, some 3 miles north of Genappe, the door was suddenly thrown open by men in high riding boots and dark green uniforms, who rushed through the three ground-floor rooms. One of them was *Fourrier du Palais* and *Adjoint du Palais de Saint Cloud* Pierre Quentin Joseph, Chevalier Baillon.

\* \* \*

Pierre Baillon had joined the army at the age of 16 as a volunteer, becoming a corporal in the Gendarmerie d'élite de la Garde on 22 March 1804, and a quartermaster in that regiment on 16 January 1805. From then on his career was closely linked to that of the Emperor, since he entered the latter's Household as a *fourrier du Palais* on 21 March 1806. In his new function he became responsible for finding suitable lodgings for the Emperor's entourage; he also had to master the facilities and etiquette of the imperial palaces, and to take responsibility for the good order, tidiness and discipline of the quarters and servants in his charge. Every morning he provided the Grand Marshal with a report on the state of the palaces, lodgings and services. He would precede the Emperor during journeys, preparing the lodgings and also cleaning them up after the entourage had left.

As a bachelor Baillon had an apartment in the Tuileries, only moving after his marriage on 22 February 1808, shortly before he was commissioned second-lieutenant in the Elite Gendarmes and left for Spain. Indeed, with the exception of the 1813 campaign, which he missed due to extreme exhaustion after the retreat from Russia, Baillon followed the Emperor on all his campaigns from 18 September 1806 until Waterloo in June 1815.

Following the First Abdication, Palace Quartermaster Baillon left his family and accompanied Napoleon to Elba; there he was given the position of Palace Prefect, and later of *adjoint du Palais* with the rank of captain from 23 July 1814. Apart from organizing receptions for visitors, he became responsible for the Emperor's campaign dressing case, the stables, and the imperial rowing boats used for inspecting the harbour and coastline; for the stables alone he had some 30 grooms, outriders, coachmen and boys under his command. Now he had returned to France to serve his emperor on campaign one last time. After the Second Abdication, promoted colonel on 21 June, he would follow Napoleon to Rochefort, begging the British to allow him to accompany the Emperor on HMS *Bellerophon*. In the family archives one reads that the Emperor, already aboard the British launch, shook his hand as one of the last, taking final leave of this faithful servant.[8]

## The night before Waterloo

On the evening of 17 June it only took a few minutes before Baillon shouted, 'The Emperor's headquarters will be here!' The farmer of Le Caillou, the 78-year-old Monsieur Boucquéau, had left his house to find refuge at the neighbouring village of Plancenoit (not the luckiest of choices, since the next evening it would become the pivot of fierce fighting between French and Prussians).

Orders were bellowed, and repeated towards the road passing the front of the house where carriages and wagons were gathering. These needed to move into the inner courtyard as quickly as possible, as more and more troops were coming up the same road towards Maison du Roi. Someone called for Capt Coignet, Wagonmaster to the Emperor; as soon as he arrived he measured the courtyard and made his dispositions for arranging the wagons. As soon as they were parked, the covers were lifted and the boxes and baggage unloaded. Everyone looked for a place out of the miserable rain where they could spend the night. Saddlers sought shelter to unload saddles and harness; farriers placed their anvils, and grooms invaded the barn looking for fodder. In the same barn the army's main ambulance unit had taken shelter, spreading straw on the floor so that they could receive and treat the wounded. Surgeons arranged and checked their instruments, pharmacists their boxes and bandages.

In no time the whole inner courtyard was transformed into a busy, crowded camp. Other carriages arrived, including those of the Emperor and the Treasury; the compound's security was under the strict control of the Elite Gendarmes commanded by Gen Radet, Grand Provost of the army. More troops arrived – the 1st Bn, 1st Foot Chasseurs of the Imperial Guard, commanded by the Dutch-born Chef de bn Duuring, responsible tonight for the perimeter protection of the 'Palace' and everyone in it.

The Household officers inspected the building and chose a room fit to receive the Emperor. The farmhouse was situated on rising ground on the east side of the Charleroi/Brussels road, and was flanked by a sheepfold, two barns and three stables. A walled orchard on the north side served as a bivouac for Duuring's Chasseurs. Once inside the building, left of the entrance, a small room (4 x 4.20m – approx.13 x 13.5ft), with a window overlooking the road, was reserved for the Emperor's ADCs, orderly officers and pages. The Emperor's own room (6.20 x 4.65m – 20.25 x 15.2ft), known as 'le salon', had two windows, one towards the road and one towards the orchard. From this one entered the dining room (6.65 x 3.80m – 21.75 x 12.3 feet).

In the meantime the cook Chandelier had commandeered the kitchen, and his mates hurried to bring in the copper and silver pans and casseroles, larding needles and supply baskets. He was not a happy man: the wagon carrying the Emperor's tableware was delayed

8 During travels in 1818–21, a disguised Baillon attempted without success to contact Napoleon's son, the Duke of Reichstadt, at Schoenbrunn. Baillon remained in touch with other faithful members of the Emperor's entourage; and during one of the sales held by the Garde-Meuble in Paris after the Second Abdication he bought the pantherskin carpet from Napoleon's campaign tent, and one of his famous hats. The carpet is now in the Army Museum, Paris, the hat in the former Brunon Collection at Château de l'Empéri, Salon de Provence.

somewhere in the rainy darkness. Shouting and swearing, he extracted from Capt Coignet a promise that someone would look for it.

The Emperor's personal valet Marchand was also missing, thanks to an accident on the choked road which had tipped his carriage over. It would take hours to repair it; arriving at Le Caillou at around 9pm, he would find the Emperor already in bed. The other valets and servants were hurrying about their individual tasks. The Emperor's room was of medium size, the ceiling supported by two beams; the walls were whitewashed, the floor tiled, and the only thing which showed a more than utilitarian elegance was the carved wooden fireplace. The sparse furniture was unceremoniously bundled out into the courtyard to make room for Napoleon's campaign pieces; the farmhouse furniture was confiscated by Duuring's soldiers or members of the Household or staff, either for their own use or for firewood to warm themselves and dry their soaking clothes.

After the room was swept clean, the bags and boxes containing furniture, equipment, maps, etc., were carried in. (At one time, at least, the camp furniture included a fully equipped lavatory, and a bath complete with heating system.) The Emperor's folding metal campaign bed, now used for the first time in this campaign, was made up and placed near the fireplace on this wet, cold night. A silver washbowl on a stand was placed in a corner, and the campaign toilet box opened on a table. The famous folding armchair with leather seat and back was placed in front of the fireplace, the portfolios arranged to ease the work of the Emperor's secretaries, and maps of the region spread out on a table.

*Fourrier du Palais* **Pierre Baillon (1776–1840). Palace quarter-masters were normally** *sous-lieutenants* **in the Elite Gendarmerie of the Imperial Guard; but Baillon, who had served Napoleon since 1806 and had followed him to Elba, was promoted colonel after the battle of Waterloo. Here he is portrayed in his crimson-faced green uniform laced with silver, complete with the pair of full epaulettes to which that rank entitled him, and the aiguillettes of the Household. The oval portrait is the original miniature from which the drawing was made. (Miniature, courtesy Musée de l'Empéri/former Brunon Collection, Salon de Provence, France; drawing, collection Paul Meganck, Brussels)**

The room was transformed from a poor farmer's parlour into the austere and efficient quarters of a conqueror – quarters reconstructed so many times before, right across Europe.

*   *   *

Following his army, at about 5.30pm the Emperor rode north with his staff and the duty squadrons along the main road, until he reached the minor crossroads and cluster of buildings at La Belle Alliance, about two miles beyond Le Caillou. From this slight rise he could dimly see Allied troops halted on Mont Saint Jean, the next gentle ridge to the north, beyond which another couple of miles took the road through Waterloo village and under the dark eaves of the Forest of Soignes. He gave his orders for the disposition of the army for the night, and returned to Le Caillou through the lashing rain. General Drouot wrote that at this stage all believed that the Allied position was simply to guard the slow retreat of their wagons and guns through the forest, and that the morning would reveal that the rest of the Allied army had followed them – there was no expectation of a general engagement on the 18th.

Chilled and soaked, the party arrived at the farm at about 8pm. Napoleon's room was not yet ready, so he lay down on a bundle of straw to warm himself at a bivouac fire. When he finally entered the farmhouse everyone except his personal attendants kept out of sight. His servants helped him out of his drenched clothes – in the case of his mud-caked boots, with some difficulty. Feeling unwell, and exhausted by his day in the saddle, he asked for his dinner to be served in his

**Le Caillou farmhouse today. Napoleon's last headquarters, on the main Brussels/Charleroi road just south of the battlefield of Waterloo, is now a museum. A plaque commemorates by name those members of the Emperor's staff who stayed there on 17/18 June 1815. (Author's collection)**

room; he ate this brief meal in bed, from the farmer's tableware, since his own still had not arrived. The Emperor's secretary Fleury de Chaboulon, looking out the window, saw a truly wretched spectacle of hungry, worn-out troops trudging through the darkness under torrential rain – infantry, cavalry, artillery and train wagons all mixed together.

In his memoirs (which are questionable at many points) Napoleon claimed to have made a late night reconnaissance; but the accounts of Gen Bernard, Marchand and Ali all agree that he did not leave his quarters that night. At about 3am he sent Col Gourgaud to reconnoitre, but it seems doubtful that he could have learned much. The Emperor passed another broken night, frequently disturbed by the coming and going of aides and messengers. (An officer of the Lancers of the Guard, a close friend and fellow countryman of Chef de bn Duuring, would later write that Napoleon was so disturbed by the noise of passing traffic that he in fact moved for part of the night to the farmhouse of Vieux Manon a little further from the road.)

## Waterloo and its aftermath

On the misty morning of Sunday 18 June 1815, the Emperor rose early. Fleury de Chaboulon wrote that it was only now that early reports confirmed that Wellington's army was drawn up in strength for battle on Mont Saint Jean. At about 8am Napoleon had breakfast with Bertrand, Soult, Duke Maret, Gen Drouot, and his younger brother Jérôme Bonaparte (the former King of Westphalia, and now commanding a division in Gen Reille's II Corps). The Emperor made a confident prediction of victory; and after the table was cleared maps were spread on it and the situation was evaluated, as continuous reports came in from officers and patrols. Then he ordered 'a well-done shoulder of mutton' for his dinner and, at some time after 9am, he mounted his mare La Marie and rode forward, accompanied by Marshal Soult, Gen Bertrand, Gen Fouler and the rest of his suite.

Napoleon went up to the advanced posts to reconnoitre the positions occupied by the enemy. He stopped for a quarter of an hour, thinking over his strategy for battle, and started giving his instructions to two generals who sat on the ground writing down his orders. He then passed through the ranks, where he was received with enthusiasm; and retired to take up position on a brow at Rosomme, west of the main road and behind the left centre of his army.

The events of the battle of Waterloo are too well known to be repeated here in any detail, though the timings given in various sources are notoriously varied. The opening cannonade was not until at least mid-morning, since hours were lost while the sun dried out the mud enough for artillery to be manoeuvred. Napoleon had not informed himself fully of the details of the battlefield; no contemporary French map or source suggests that his staff were even aware that Hougoumont, hidden in its woods, was a substantial building, strongly garrisoned by the British as the anchor of the Allied right flank.

The most basic orders given by the Major-General, Marshal Soult, to the various corps commanders were remarkably vague from the outset. Notoriously, he sent Marshal Ney a page torn from his notebook stating that at about 1pm the attack should begin on Mont Saint Jean (which he wrongly believed to be a village) and the crossroads situated there; that Gen d'Erlon's I Corps (on the right or east of the road) should open this attack, with his left-hand division forward and the others supporting it; and that Gen Reille's II Corps (on the left or west of the road) should advance level with d'Erlon to guard his flank. Ney – whose relationship with Soult was poisonous – may have been deliberately mischievous when he added in pencil that 'Count d'Erlon understands that the attack is to be opened on the left rather than the right' and that this 'new disposition' should be communicated to Reille. In other words, Ney at least pretended to be confused over whether Soult meant that the attack should be opened by the left wing *of I Corps*, or the left wing *of the whole army*. Reille did not share this confusion; but there would be a number of others more damaging during the course of the day.

After the battle, Gen Flahaut wrote that few of the orders written by Marshal Soult carried the time that the order was sent. (This was a major shortcoming, which would have been unthinkable in Berthier's time: he always added the name of the officer who carried the message, the hour and place where it was written and sent. When he was interrupted while writing an order, he would even insert the exact time when he recommenced.)

At 1.30pm, Soult sent a message to Marshal Grouchy, whose detached corps were trying to keep contact with the Prussians off to the north-east. By now the first reports had already reached Napoleon of troop movements to the east of Wellington's line, which would turn out to be the first of Blücher's troops coming to his aid; Grouchy was already too late to get between the two Allied armies. Soult's despatch to Grouchy did not reach him until about 5.00pm; written in pencil, it was almost illegible. Grouchy read it as saying *'La bataille est gagnée...* (the battle has been won)', instead of *'La bataille est engagée...* (the battle has started)'. Some of Grouchy's generals had been urging him to march west towards the sounds of battle; but the marshal's last written orders from Napoleon had been to attack Wavre – which he was still doing the next morning, when the battle of Waterloo had been lost and Emperor and army were in full retreat.

At around 3pm or 4pm – the period of the afternoon when Napoleon passed tactical command to Marshal Ney for a renewed attack in the centre, with such disastrous results – the Emperor asked for something to eat. His Mameluke Ali returned to Le Caillou to tell Pierron, the majordomo, to bring food for the Emperor and some of his suite. As he went towards the farm he later remembered that bullets were flying over his head from the direction of the Prussians arriving on the east of the battlefield – and that this fire was a good deal heavier on his way back to the Emperor.

\*　　\*　　\*

The chaotic situation of the French retreat that night forced the Emperor to seek protection in the square of the 1st Foot Grenadiers of the Guard opposite Le Caillou, where he was found by his ADC Gen Flahaut when the latter returned from charging with the cavalry. Escorted from the field by Gen Bertrand, Marshal Soult, Gen Drouot, his brother Prince Jérôme, Gen Colbert, Gen Morand, Gen de Labédoyère and Flahaut, Napoleon hoped to find his *dormeuse* coach at the farm, since their riding horses were exhausted. However, Gen Fouler, the acting Grand Equerry, had already sent the carriages towards Genappe, keeping a *brigade* of fresh horses near the farm, under the supervision of the page Gudin and some outriders. These ten remounts would allow the Emperor to find safety eventually at Philippeville, some 25 miles away. Flahaut recalled in a letter that the Emperor was so exhausted that he fell asleep in the saddle, riding knee to knee with Flahaut.

The fresh horses took them first to Genappe, where they found the Emperor's carriage; but the press of traffic was so chaotic that it had to be left behind in order to escape the pursuing Prussian cavalry. The valet Marchand, who had accompanied the Emperor's carriages, found the crossroads at Quatre-Bras blocked by fleeing troops. At Le Caillou, afraid of looters, he had already taken 300,000 francs in banknotes and hidden them under his clothes; now he went through the rest of the Emperor's belongings in order to save what was possible, but the approach of Prussian troopers forced him to flee. The Grand Provost, Baron Radet, wounded by shell splinters in the knee and hip, tried with Gen Neigre to restore some order and save the Emperor's baggage train; but he was overwhelmed by the masses of fleeing French troops, and knocked unconscious.

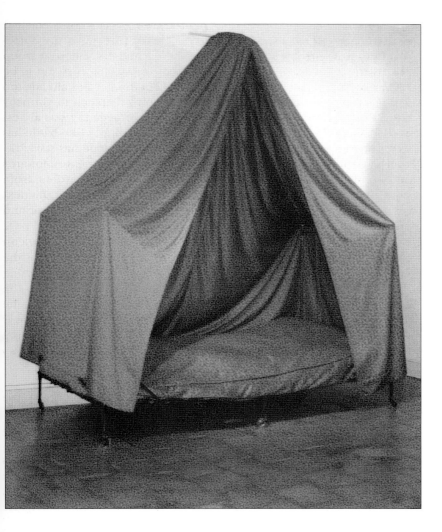

One of Napoleon's famous metal folding camp beds, made by Desouches. This one has a green silk canopy, and may be considered as the *'grand lit'*; a second, without a canopy, was known as the *'petit lit'*. (Author's collection)

At about 5am on the morning of 19 June the Emperor and his small party arrived at Philippeville, where the exhausted Napoleon rested in a room at a shabby inn – Au Lion d'Or. His Mameluke half-undressed him and he went to bed; according to Ali, the Emperor was depressed and absorbed in thought. Gradually more members of his entourage arrived; the party now included Marshal Soult, Gens Bertrand, Drouot, Flahaut, Corbineau, Labedoyère, Equerry Canisy, Duke Maret, Col Belly de Bussy, the secretary Fleury de Chaboulon and the page Gudin. While the Emperor and his staff ate some bread with a few eggs, he received the local military commander Gen Dupuy de Saint Florent, Major Casergue, the sub-prefect and the mayor.

After giving some instructions and discussing the situation with his officers, Napoleon and his party left for Laon at around 1pm, in three carriages with an escort of some 200 troopers. They halted around 5pm on the 19th at Senses-Corbineau, where the Emperor asked the local priest, Abbé Herisson, what he thought at seeing him there; to this the priest replied, 'I would rather see you on the other side of the Rhine, Sire.'

The next day they halted at Mézières to change horses, but these were not available for some hours. General Dumonceau, commander of the 2nd Military Division, and the local commander – an officer named Traulle – gathered with their staffs around the carriages; only the Grand Marshal, Bertrand, got out. Traulle recalled that there were no escorts apart from one senior officer in hussar uniform; and that all the curtains of the carriages were closed.

At Laon the Emperor wrote his last Bulletin; and at 11pm that night, 20 June, accompanied by Bertrand and Ali, he left for Paris. After a long night's journey along bumpy roads the Emperor's carriage reached the Elysée Palace at 6am on the 21st. General Caulaincourt was there to welcome him; the Emperor was very tired and short of breath, and – pressing one hand over his heart – asked for a few hours' rest before he addressed state affairs. Two days later, on 22 June 1815, the Emperor signed his second and final abdication.

## SELECT BIBLIOGRAPHY

Archives in the library of the Belgian Royal Army Museum, Brussels

Bucquoy, Cdt, *Les uniformes du 1er Empire: La Maison de l'Empereur,* J.Grancher, Paris (1977)
Elting, John R., *Swords Around a Throne,* Phoenix, London (1999)
Lechartier, G., *Les Services de l'arrière à la Grande Armée en 1806–1807,* Chapelot, Paris (1910)
Mansel, Philip, *The Eagle in Splendour, Napoleon I and his Court,* George Philip, London (1987)
Pigeard, Alain, *Dictionnaire de la Grande Armée,* Tallandier, Paris (2002)
Quintin, Danielle & Bernard, *Dictionnaire des Colonels de Napoléon,* SPM, Paris (1996)
Rogers, H.C.B., *Napoleon's Army,* Ian Allan Ltd, Shepperton, Surrey (1974)

Magazines: *Tradition, Soldats Napoléoniens, La Revue Napoléon* – various issues

# THE PLATES

## A: ORDERLY OFFICERS TO THE EMPEROR; ELBA, 1814

In May 1814 there were six orderly officers on Elba, all *sous-lieutenants*, specially commissioned from among local citizens. In August 1814, *Chef d'escadron* of Gendarmerie Jacques Roul joined this small staff; he would be the only orderly officer to follow Napoleon when he returned to France.

The uniforms on this plate are reconstructed from the official decree that created the post; note the crimson-white cockade worn on Elba. The all-green uniforms were very simple when compared with the previous design of sky-blue with silver embroidery. Note the silver turn-back device of a bee, a Bonapartist symbol retained by Napoleon from the days of his former dignity. The sabres were not covered by the regulations; neither is anything said about the saddle or saddlecloth, although mounted duties were an important part of the orderly officer's service.

**A1: Regulation full dress, mounted**
**A2: Full dress, unmounted, summer**
The loose white cotton trousers were non-regulation, but a normal concession in the hot Mediterranean climate.

**A3: Evening dress**
Based on the regulation uniform, this young officer follows the height of fashion for 1814, which was suitable for evening dress. The large hat is of the Russian style; the waist of the jacket is cut very high, as is the waistcoat, giving an elegant 'short chest'.

## B: POSTILIONS OF THE IMPERIAL HOUSEHOLD & HEADQUARTERS

The drivers *(postillons)* of the Household and of the Imperial Headquarters rode the teams not only of the Emperor's coaches but of all the carriages of the various members of the staff and Household. Their picturesque appearance, including the archaic wig and the jacket with exaggeratedly short-cut tails, is very typical of coach drivers during the French Empire. Note the enormous boots (copied from

**Louis Honoré Richebé (1787–1814) was appointed an ADC to Marshal Mortier on 10 September 1811. Here he is seen in the uniform of an officer serving as ADC to a marshal who was not a prince: a dark blue hussar-style uniform with a fur *colback*. Richebé would only serve in this function for a brief period, but was active in Napoleon's armies throughout the Empire. He was killed near Paris on 30 March 1814, as *Chef de bataillon major* of the Regiment of Chasseurs-Flanqueurs of the Imperial Guard. (Courtesy Musée de l'Empéri/former Brunon Collection, Salon de Provence, France)**

originals in the Musée de la Poste in Paris); intended to protect the legs from crushing while riding in the team, they made walking virtually impossible – the drivers often kept their shoes on inside the boots and slipped out of them when dismounted. Note (**B2**) the special stirrups, adapted to the dimensions of the boots. We read that sometimes drivers or couriers had been riding for so long that they were unable to dismount; to save every moment at relay stations they were lifted from the horse complete with the saddle, and a fresh mount was guided under them. The uniform, always proudly worn, is in the imperial livery of green and red with gold lace; the yellow lace on the round hat was also a special feature. The plaque worn on the left arm indicated a professional driver. The brass badge with a crowned eagle, worn on the breast, identified a 'diploma'd' courier, – a mission to which Headquarters drivers were sometimes allocated.

In the background is a typical early 19th century coach, which could be either one of the Emperor's or one used by his staff. During the period of the Empire, most French coaches were traditionally painted with yellow bodies and red chassis and wheels; but we know that Napoleon used several of other colours, blue or green. All the coaches of the Headquarters bore, as here, the imperial coat of arms on the doors.

## C: VALETS TO THE EMPEROR

Due to their memoirs, the Emperor's personal body servants Constant Wairy and Louis Marchand are well known; but there were, of course, numerous other valets in the Household who followed the Emperor on campaign and fulfilled various duties at his Headquarters. Not surprisingly, there are very few pictorial records of these servants; but original documents such as invoices from merchants allow us to reconstruct the several costumes which they wore according to circumstances and instructions. For most occasions they displayed the imperial livery of green and red with gold lace. From our sources we can extract three main orders of dress: the grand livery, worn only for palace duty; the full livery, and the small livery. For daily duty and on campaign, all these uniforms had gilt buttons with a crowned eagle. We illustrate here the full and small liveries, the only orders of dress worn by servants on campaign.

### C1: Small livery; campaign dress, c.1805–07

This costume is partly seen as Plate B4 in Part 1 of this study, Elite 115, as worn by Constant. It is a simplified version of full livery, with a stand-and-fall collar and without lace on the back of the coat; in contrast to the figure of Constant, this ordinary butler has no gold lace on the pocket flaps, in keeping with his lower rank. We have given him a hat, an alternative to the often-illustrated 'jockey cap'; the shape of this hat and the cut of the coat would date this valet to around 1805–07. Before 1808, only a plain hat was worn with the small livery. A painting by Lejeune does not show side buttons on the green pantaloons. We do not know the details of the waistcoat at this date, but assume that it was the same as in later years – scarlet, with a double row of gilt buttons.

### C2 & C3: Full livery; campaign dress, 1804–15

A gold-laced cocked hat which accompanied the full livery was not worn when on service close to the Emperor. These valets are on evening service in the presence of the Emperor, on which occasions they always wore powdered hair, even on campaign. The full livery coat, cut '*à la francaise*', is reconstructed after various sources. The pantaloons were red during the Consulate period but became green with the creation of the Empire, probably as early as 1804. The waistcoat should have been scarlet with doubled gold lace, narrow on the inside front and bordering the pockets. In **summer dress (C2)** the coat remained the same but the pantaloons should have been of pale yellow 'nankin', and the vest of a white lightweight cotton called *basin* – the latter, according to our sources, without lace. Boots were always worn for travelling and on campaign. Out of doors in **winter dress (C4)**, the 'jockey cap' was worn, and the *carrick* – a long, generously cut caped riding mantle with a double collar, and sleeves long enough to cover the hands.

## D: MILITARY POSTAL SERVICE & SPECIAL COURIER

Inside the borders of the empire, military correspondence was assured through the garrison offices of the towns; but for the army in the field, from 1809, a specialized service was organized to transmit letters, despatches and – not least – funds. This Military Postal Service was entirely staffed by civilians, including the most senior personnel, but under the command of the military administration authorities (*intendants général, commissaires-ordonnateurs* and *commissaires des guerres*). The service comprised two divisions: one for correspondence and funds, and one for materials, coaches and limbers. In each army there was a *grand bureau* at army HQ and a divisional bureau in each army corps HQ. When the Emperor was commanding the army in person, the director-in-chief of the Military Postal Service would come under the orders of the Grand Marshal of the Palace.

Normal correspondence was transported by ordinary professional couriers, by coach or on horseback, often escorted by professional guards. Escorted limbers usually transported the funds. Urgent and confidential despatches were carried by special couriers; these were attached to each army and army corps, and the Emperor had his own.

In the background of this plate we show – after an ink drawing by Swebach – a two-wheel coach as usually used for transport of letters; the packs are on the roof, protected by a '*soufflet*' of oilcloth.

### D1: Inspector-in-chief, Military Postal Service, 1809–15

The uniform once again shows the imperial colours of green and red. The tail turn-backs bore silver embroidered stars and three embroidered buttonholes; the latter were also seen on the collar, cuffs and horizontal pockets.

### D2: Sub-employee, Military Postal Service

These were used to escort couriers, coaches and limbers of the service. Note the two holstered pistols on his belt; and just visible are the red five-point stars on the coat turn-backs.

### D3: Courier, Military Postal Service

A characteristic detail of the uniform is the plain silver laced buttonholes on the collar and cuffs; he too has red stars on his turn-backs. The special silver badge on the left breast shows a crowned eagle with the inscription '*POSTE MILITAIRE*' in a half-circle.

### D4: 'Moustache', First Courier to the Emperor, 1804–06

One of Napoleon's personal couriers was Jacques Chazal,

who became famous by his nickname 'Moustache'. The Emperor had total confidence in Chazal, and confided special messages to him. He appears in a painting of Bonaparte's entry into Antwerp, 1803, by the Belgian painter M.I.Van Bree, which now hangs in Versailles. Today we can put a name to the figure, since we have found some wonderful preparation sketches for the painting in the Louvre, Paris. The small badge on the lapel of his coat indicates his special status: it shows an eagle with, probably, the inscription *'COURRIER DU PREMIER CONSUL'* in a half-circle above – later to be changed to *'COURRIER DE L'EMPEREUR'*.

## E: POSTAL SERVICE & COURIERS
### E1: Imperial courier, c.1804–06
Also after a painting by M.I.Van Bree, this uniform is essentially the same as that worn by 'Moustache' opposite, but simpler and with much less gold lace embellishment.
### E2: General Headquarters courier, c.1806–07
After the Zimmermann MS. Such couriers were to be seen around the Army General Headquarters and at every other headquarters in the service of the generals commanding armies. The crossed lapels, even at this late date, seem to be a characteristic of the couriers' uniforms – see Plates D4 & E1. For some reason the breast badge is worn here on the right-hand side.

### E3: Driver, Imperial Postal Service, c.1810–12
An ordinary postilion of the Imperial Mail, on temporary duty near the Imperial Headquarters – it was not unusual for personnel of the ordinary civilian mail service to be taken from their daily duties for temporary service around the headquarters. Our figure wears his usual uniform, but the

**Self-portrait of Baron Lejeune as ADC to Marshal Berthier. This shows *Chef d'escadron* Lejeune in the uniform worn before this soldier-artist designed the better-known outfit of white, scarlet and black (see Elite 115, page 17; and Elite 72, Plate K2) for the Major-General's aides. Berthier was made Prince of Neuchâtel in late 1805; the lake in the background probably dates this portrait to around spring 1806. Lejeune's uniform consists of a sky-blue pelisse with brown fur trim, sky-blue trousers and a red dolman, all with silver lace and embroidery, and a black shako with a white plume; the hussar-style shabraque is of pantherskin. (Courtesy Musée de l'Empéri/former Brunon Collection, Salon de Provence, France)**

tricolour ribbons on his round hat indicate his temporary attachment. It was normal for drivers to keep their own stirrups, for ease in frequent and rapid changing of horses; like the massive protective boots, the stirrups were made to their personal measurements.

## F: ARMY GENERAL HEADQUARTERS PERSONNEL

As mentioned in Elite 115, Marshal Berthier, as the Major-General of the Grande Armée (i.e. Chief of the General Staff), took pains to ensure that his own staff and troops at GHQ were distinguished by special uniforms. Like a true *seigneur* of the *Ancien Régime,* the Prince of Neuchâtel took a close interest in the appearance of his followers, both military and civilian.

### F1: Grenadier, Bataillon de Neuchâtel, 1806–12
After the Würtz Collection. We learn from the memoirs of Napoleon's secretary, Baron Fain, that Berthier always had a company of grenadiers from his Bataillon de Neuchâtel to guard his HQ. The yellow coats worn by these Swiss troops were well known throughout the army, and the unit was nicknamed *'les serins'* – a popular French term for canaries. As was the norm in the French Army, the grenadiers were distinguished by fringed red epaulettes, and red braid, cords and plumes on the headdress.

### F2: Courier to the Major-General, c.1807–09
A contemporary picture of this special GHQ courier shows these unusual boots, with large protective feet (cf the postilions' boots on previous plates) but normally proportioned shafts. The red of this uniform was probably considered as Berthier's livery colour, since it was also worn by his ADCs. Note the brassard of red edged with blue and bearing an eagle badge.

### F3: Guide-interpreter of the Army of Germany, 1805
This short-lived special unit of two squadrons, raised from

German-speakers to serve as headquarters couriers and orderly officers, is described in Elite 115. White was another uniform colour favoured by Berthier for his personal troops.

## G: GUIDES OF THE PRINCE OF NEUCHÂTEL

This company – also known simply as the *Guides de Berthier*, and, at least temporarily, as the *Compagnie d'élite du grand quartier général* – was formed in 1807 by amalgamating the former *Guides Interprètes* of the Armies of England and Germany (see Elite 115). They carried out all kinds of guard and escort duties for the Army General Headquarters; trusted veterans, the Guides followed Berthier on all his campaigns from 1807 to 1814, in Germany, Poland, Austria, Russia – where they were virtually wiped out – and France.

### G1: Officer, daily uniform, c.1807–10

This was the original uniform: all green, and worn with the fur busby or *colback*.

### G2: Guide, Compagnie d'élite du grand quartier général, c.1810–11

After the manuscript of Otto von Bade. It was probably in 1810 that the uniform changed to this version, with white lapels and red facings and turn-backs. The Guides of Berthier were seen as dragoons, so we may suppose that the Major-General favoured the idea of uniforming them as a *compagnie d'élite*, with the distinctions of such companies within the line dragoon regiments.

### G3: Guide, 1814

The uniform of the Guides of Berthier after the 1812 Bardin regulations. It is a mixture of line and Guard dragoon features, and that was certainly the desired impression.

### H: The Emperor's tented camp, Russia, 1812

This is reconstructed after the 1812 decree on the composition of the Emperor's train, now in the Caulaincourt papers in the National Archives, Paris – see plan view on page 41 for key.

# INDEX